AND ON THE SIXTH DAY...

A MUSICAL DRAMA

by

Jack Sharkey and Dave Reiser

SAMUEL FRENCH, INC.
45 West 25th Street   NEW YORK 10001
7623 Sunset Boulevard HOLLYWOOD 90046
LONDON   TORONTO

MUSIC—IMPORTANT

A piano/vocal score is available on receipt of the following:

1. **$25.00 deposit, which is refunded on return to us of the material in good condition immediately following your production, plus first class postage.**
2. **A non-refundable rental fee of $15.00 for each performance planned.**
3. **Number of performances and exact performance dates.**
4. **$3.00 to cover postage and handling.**

We cannot fill any order for music unless it is accompanied by remittance as above, as all rental material is handled on a strictly C.O.D. basis.

CAST OF CHARACTERS

NOTE: *Each* role in this musical may be played by a different individual. However, for groups wishing smaller casts, we have broken the cast of characters down into an easily doubled-up cast of 10 players, 5 men and 5 women, making full allowance for costume-changes between the various scenes, etc. Male roles are numbered 1-through-five, female roles indicated A-through-E.

1. VOICE OF GOD (only unseen player) - MOSES
2. SATAN
3. ADAM - ABRAHAM - ESAU - JOSHUA - DAVID - BARBER
4. NOAH - LOT - SAMSON - DANIEL - JOSEPH - MYRMIDON
5. ISAAC - JACOB - JONAH - URIAH - BARBER

A. EVE - SARAH - DELILAH - BATHSHEBA
B. NOAH'S WIFE - JONAH'S WIFE - MARY
C. LOT'S WIFE - JONAH'S MOTHER-IN-LAW - LIONESS
D. LIONESS - HANDMAIDEN TO DELILAH
E. LIONESS - HANDMAIDEN TO BATHSHEBA

CHORUS parts are played by those performers who are not playing principals in each scene.

SPECIAL NOTE: If male player #5 cannot negotiate the boyish vocal range for young ISAAC, and sound like a young boy, then this role should be played by female player D or E; the piping voice of a happy young boy is essential to the proper sound of his duet with much-older ABRAHAM.

AND ON THE
SIXTH DAY...

MUSICAL NUMBERS

ACT ONE — CREATION-OVERTURE

Scene 1: GARDEN OF EDEN
"It's Boring" .... God, Adam
"Why Shouldn't You Eat the Apple?". .... Satan
"If You Love Me" .... Eve, Adam

Scene 2: THE FLOOD
"Rain! Rain! .... Noah, Wife

Scene 3: THE PROMISE
"We're Gonna Have a Baby!" .... Abraham, Sarah, Satan
"Up to the Mountain". .... Abraham, Isaac

Scene 4: SODOM AND GOMORRAH
"Don't Look Back" [Where's the Harm?] .... Lot,
Chorus [Satan]

Scene 5: A COZY KITCHEN
[no musical number] .... Jacob, Esau

Scene 6: THE EXODUS
"Why Should You Obey the Commandments?" .... Satan
"Orgy Time!" .... Chorus

Scene 7: JERICHO
"Blow That Trumpet!". .... Satan, Chorus

ACT TWO — ENTR'ACTE — PASSAGE OF THE YEARS

Scene 1: THE VALLEY OF SORECH
"Samson, Dear"/"Allegory" .... Samson, Delilah
"Delilah". .... Barbershop Quartet

Scene 2: A COTTAGE BY THE SEA*
[no musical number]. .... Wife, Mother, Husband

Scene 3: A ROYAL PALACE
"Hey, Bathsheba!" .... Bathsheba
"Dance of Temptation"/"Uriah's Doom". .... David, Uriah
"It Is Done"/"What Have I Done?" .... David, Bathsheba

Scene 4: DOWN IN THE DEN
"Daniel's Answer" [Roar, Lions, Roar!]. .... Daniel
[Satan, Lionesses]

Scene 5: BETHLEHEM
"Lullaby" [Why Should You Adore The Infant?]. .... Chorus
[Satan]

*[IMPORTANT: "Cottage" scene should be program-listed *exactly* as above, without character-names cited, or the punchline of the scene won't pay off during a performance, if husband-name is known.]

AND ON THE SIXTH DAY... had its world premiere at Altergott Auditorium in Palatine, Illinois on June 14, 1983, with the following cast and crew:

VOICE OF GOD .... Phil Ridarelli
VOICE OF GOD II, JOSHUA, MYRMIDON .... Jim Kelly
ADAM, LOT, BARBER .... Skip Martin
EVE, DELILAH .... Laura Daugherty
NOAH, URIAH, JOSEPH .... John Lundin
NOAH'S WIFE, LIONESS .... Marianne Nance
ABRAHAM, "HUSBAND" .... John Ector
SARAH, HANDMAIDEN, MARY .... Missy Neargarder
ISAAC, "WIFE," LIONESS .... Colleen Carey
"MOTHER," LIONESS .... LouAnn Corey
ESAU, SAMSON, DANIEL .... Dave Bazant
JACOB, KING DAVID, BARBER .... Dave Huter
LOT'S WIFE, BATHSHEBA .... Tammy Jackson
SATAN .... Rob Howell

DIRECTOR - Rob Howell
TECHNICAL DIRECTOR - Greg Thomas
LIGHTS - Dave Wicklund and Lisa Howell
MUSICAL DIRECTOR - David Reiser
ACCOMPANIST - Camille Jacobsen
CHOREOGRAPHY - Missy Neargarder and Laura Daugherty
(Bathsheba's dance choreographed by
Karen Grisco and Tammy Jackson)
STAGE CREW - Jim Forman, Jody Epstein
Larry Moore and Karen Meinort
POSTER/PROGRAM-ART/DESIGN - Lisa Obara

★ ★ ★ ★ ★ ★ ★ ★ ★ ★ ★ ★ ★

NOTE: As you can see, the premiere group opted to divide the cast-members differently from the suggested role-assignments; feel free to do the same, according to the needs and/or desires of your own theatre group.

Audience-response to the premiere was ecstatic, and the show played to a packed house for its entire run. Here is a cross-section sampling of comments by first-nighters after the show:

"I've always puzzled over the Esau-and-Jacob story, wondering why God chose Jacob to be the father of the Twelve Tribes after the dirty trick he played on his father. Now it's all very clear to me.... The end of the Creation scene was so meaningful to me as a parent — God punished Adam and Eve not because he disliked them but because he loved them."

—Bea Schonta, Palatine

"Very reverent and lots of fun, too."

—Alec Margate, Mount Prospect

"My children learned more about the Bible tonight than they've learned in six years of Bible School!"

—Emmy Quade, Arlington Heights

"I never thought a musical based upon Bible stories could be so entertaining. I'm very impressed."

—Leonard Wattly, DesPlaines

" 'Lullaby' is the most beautiful Christmas Carol I've ever heard. It should be published separately."

—Lainie Johnson, Rolling Meadows

"My granddaughter, Nicole — she'll be two in September — was completely involved and sat quietly through the whole play. When the apple came down, she asked, "What's that?" When God would speak, she'd point up and ask, "Who's that?" She really enjoyed every minute."

—Mrs. William Wagner, Chicago

"I thought it was just wonderful. All my friends enjoyed it. They're going to tell their friends about it so they can come, too."

—Mary Luckey, Oak Park

"...thoroughly delightful musical comedy. We want to see it again."
—Bill & Catherine Rose, Elmwood Park

"Amusing but reverent portrayal of Bible History. The show is a gem."
—Phyllis O'Keefe, DesPlaines

"A joy to behold. I loved the crisp, witty dialogue. The show abounds with hilarious lines."

—Dellora Johnson, Chicago

"Jack Sharkey is surely the best author of stage humor today. I have laughed through six of his comedies, and found this one the most delightful of all."
—Gladys Kugel, St. Joseph, Michigan

"Those writers have a gift for taking a grave topic and treating it with reverent and hearty humor. We loved every moment."
—Kathy & Geoff Thornley, Park Ridge

"Dave Reiser and Jack Sharkey brought us hours of sheer enjoyment tonight ... captivating songs and hilarious dialogue ... looking forward to seeing more of their shows!"

—Ceil & Clem McDermott, River Forest

[ARTWORK for posters/program/publicity]

AND ON THE
SIXTH DAY...

ACT ONE
Scene One

When house lights dim to black, curtain opens in darkness. Then "Creation-Overture" begins:

GOD. Let there be light!

(Music starts, stage lights [this never includes the backdrop] come up to half-full at end of music.)

GOD. Let the waters appear, and the heavens above the waters!

(Sound of seaside surf begins, stage lights come up to three-quarters full during music.)

GOD. Let there be dry land amid the waters and all manner of vegetation upon the land!

(During music, backdrop comes up to half-full, and projects a phantasmagoria of leaves, vines, etc.)

GOD. Let there be lights in the heavens, and changes of seasons, and a sun to rule the heavens by day, and a moon and stars to rule the heavens by night!

(During music, stage lights and backdrop come up to full.)

God. Let there be living creatures in the waters—

(A bubbling sound joins the music.)

God. —and living creatures moving through the air!

(A birdsong sound joins bubbling sound and music.)

God. Let there be creatures upon the land—

(One-by-one, we hear animal sounds joining preceding sounds during music — lowing cattle, roaring lions, chittering monkeys, etc. etc. — at appropriate moments during remainder of speech and completion of overture.)

God. —cattle and beasts of the field, and wild beasts in the forests and jungles and in the trees and upon the ground, and each of them male and female of their kind!

(As overture ends, all sounds fade to silence.)

God. There, it's done!

God #2. *(Note: This is the voice of the same player, with just slightly altered inflection, to sound like the same speaker but slightly different.)* It's a magnificent job, Father. An entire universe in just six days! What made you decide to create it?

God. Well, Son, I'm sure you remember a short while back, when I was saying— *(Sings.)*
IT'S BORING — ONLY ME IN ETERNITY, IT'S BORING.
I THINK I'LL TRY MY HAND, FOR WHAT IT'S WORTH,
AND MAKE SOME SEA AND LAND AND CALL IT "EARTH."

God #2. Yes, I remember. And I remember arguing the point with you, too. After all, you're not alone in eternity. You have me, and we have our Spirit of the love we bear one another.

God. Yes, but you and I and the Spirit are one. We know each other completely. It would be nice, I think, to have some other persons about, who could learn all about us. And that's why—
(Sings.)

IT'S BORING — PLEASANT SIGHT, BUT IT'S NOT QUITE
RIGHT,
IT'S BORING.
ANOTHER CREATURE'S NEEDED HERE, I GUESS;
A PERSON JUST LIKE ME — WELL, MORE OR LESS.
    GOD #2. Well, then, why not create one?
    GOD. All right. There!

(Hedges slide onstage from left and right.)

    GOD #2. Where?
    GOD. Here he comes, right now!
    ADAM. *(Enters from right; the hedge is just up to his chest-height, hiding
the rest of him.)* Hello, up there!
    GOD. Hello, Adam. How are you enjoying Paradise?
    ADAM. *(Sings.)*
IT'S BORING — PARADISE SHOULD BE TWICE AS NICE,
IT'S BORING.
    GOD. *(Sings.)*
HE'S LONESOME, I CAN SEE, SO I'LL CREATE
A FEMALE OF HIS SPECIES FOR A MATE.
(spoken) Adam — go to sleep.

(ADAM closes his eyes, sinks from view.)

    GOD. There. Now, I'll just take some bone of his bone and flesh
of his flesh—
    GOD #2. Why are you taking it from that particular area,
Father?
    GOD. So that the new creature — like unto the area chosen —
will be closest to his heart. There, it's done. Adam, wake up!
    ADAM. *(Comes into view again.)* That was a nice rest, Lord. Thanks.
But — I seem to have lost something!
    GOD. No, actually, you have gained something. Another
human being to be a companion to you.

(EVE enters from left; the hedge is neck-high on her.)

God. Here she is, now.

Adam. *(Looks at her quietly, then looks heavenward.)*
Is this a rib?

Eve. Adam, I know you're the first man — but did that have to be the first joke?

Adam. Sorry. Say — what's your name?

Eve. You decide.

Adam. I think I'll call you "Eve." It's a pretty name, for a lovely lady.

Eve. Okay. Say — what is this place we're in, anyhow?

Adam. It's called Paradise. Would you like a tour of the premises?

Eve. Sure thing.

(They exit, right.)

God #2. Well, Father, are you contented now?

God. Not quite. They like me, I'm sure. But they haven't had much of a chance *not* to. What I'd like is for them to have options — to choose Me, or choose something else — and then choose Me. It's no fun being loved if the lover has no other choice.

God #2. Then you're not content with creation yet?

God. No, not quite. It's— *(Sings.)*
*STILL BORING — I KNOW SIN IS WHAT I HAVE BEEN
IGNORING.
IT MIGHT MESS UP CREATION, BUT I'D BEST
ALLOW SOME SMALL TEMPTATION AS A TEST.*
(Calls.) Adam! Eve!

(They re-enter.)

Adam. Yes, Lord?

Eve. Was there something you wanted?

God. I'd like to show you something.

(An apple descends from above them, stops just over head-height, hanging there, bright and attractive.)

GOD. Do you see this fruit?

ADAM. Yes, Lord.

EVE. It looks absolutely delicious!

GOD. Well — I have a request. You two may eat of any of the fruit that grows in the garden — except for this one. Is it a deal?

ADAM. Of course it is.

GOD. Eve?

EVE. Well — yes — of course ... but it certainly looks delicious.... Oh, well, a deal's a deal! Come on, Adam, let's go see some more of the animals. By the way — why did you call that big fat one a hippopotamus?

ADAM. *(Shrugs.)* It *looks* like a hippopotamus...?!

(They exit.)

GOD #2. There, now, are you satisfied?

GOD. Yes, I guess I am.

(SATAN enters from left, in front of hedge; he is lithe and wiry of build, wearing black: shoes, socks, slacks and turtleneck sweater.)

SATAN. You call that a test?!

GOD. Yes, I do. They had a choice, and they chose correctly.

SATAN. Ten seconds! That's all the time it took! Ten seconds! But how about if the temptation lasted a little longer?

GOD. You're up to something.

SATAN. Of course! I'm *always* up to something. I don't like to see so much happiness. It hurts. If *I'm* spending an eternity of misery, it doesn't seem fair to have *other* creatures having a good time.

GOD. I offered you heaven. Misery was your own choice.

SATAN. That's because you were so bossy. I'd rather rule in hell than be a servant in heaven!

GOD. I didn't ask you to be my servant, only my friend.

SATAN. Sure, that's what you *said.* But I know you must have had some kind of sneaky angle. That's why I moved out.

GOD. I don't have sneaky angles.

SATAN. *Everyone's* got an angle!

God. And you didn't move — you were evicted. Why must you always lie?

Satan. I hate the truth. The truth hurts. I just wanted to be left alone!

God. And I gave you what you wanted. Apart from me, the Creator, there can be nothing but aloneness.

Satan. You didn't give it! I took it!

God. I won't argue the point.

Satan. Good! If you'll pardon the expression. Now, about these two little wimps you just created — how about you let me lay a *real* temptation on them?

God. But they're so happy. I'd rather let them stay that way.

Satan. Can't take the competition, huh? Don't trust your own creatures, huh? Afraid of what they'll do if you give 'em the chance, huh?

God. No. I know what will happen. But I leave you your choice.

Satan. Oh, sure, easy for you to say! Because you *know* if they get one look at me, they'll be horrified, and won't listen to a word I say! I'll need a disguise!

God. I give you permission. Do what you will.

Satan. Now you're talking! Let me see— *(Moves to left side of stage.)* —I saw one of those dinosaurs over here — maybe he'll let me use his body for a few minutes...

God. If he does, he will be violating my intentions. By helping you, he will condemn his entire species.

Satan. Ha! You'll wipe him out, huh! And all his kind! That's the kind of loving creator *you* are.

God. No, I won't wipe him out. But his descendants will all eat dust for all their lives, in reminder of what he has done, and crawl upon the ground instead of walking.

Satan. Quiet! He'll hear you! *(Reaches offstage.)* Hi, friend! Let me just borrow your body for a moment! *(His hand brings in top half of serpent-head — top of skull, eyes, nostrils and upper fangs — which he then places, cap-fashion, atop his head.)* There! All disguised. Now, where is that woman-creature?

(EVE enters, alone, stands looking up at apple.)

SATAN. Ah, there she is! Now to get to work! Hi, there, lady!

EVE. Oh! I thought I was alone! Good morning to you, serpent.

SATAN. Admiring that fruit, are you? And well you should! It's quite the most delicious fruit in the garden.

EVE. You've tasted it? I thought it was forbidden?

SATAN. Only to you and Adam. The rest of the creatures eat all they want.

EVE. That doesn't seem fair.

SATAN. And it's not! Why don't you take a big bite, right now?

EVE. Oh, how I'd love to—! But — no — I shouldn't even think about it!

SATAN. *(Sings.)*

WHY SHOULDN'T YOU EAT THE APPLE?
WHY SHOULDN'T YOU TASTE ITS MEAT?
I KNOW YOU EXPECT IT'LL BE SO DELECTABLE,
JUICY, AND CRUNCHY AND SWEET!
WHY SHOULDN'T YOU EAT THE APPLE?
WHY SHOULD YOU BE SO DEPRIVED?
DON'T BE SUCH A FOOL, IT'S A SILLY OLD RULE
THAT THE GUY IN THE SKY HAS CONTRIVED!

EVE. I can't!

SATAN. *(Sings.)*

C'MON, BE BRAVE, YOU HAVE THE RIGHT
TO GET SOME ENJOYMENT IN LIFE!
BE SURE TO SAVE A LITTLE BITE
FOR ADAM FROM HIS LOVING WIFE!
WHY SHOULDN'T YOU EAT THE APPLE?
WHAT'S WRONG WITH A LITTLE TASTE?
YOU KNOW, ANYHOW, IF YOU DON'T EAT IT NOW
IT'LL SHRIVEL AND JUST GO TO WASTE!

EVE. What a shame!

SATAN. *(Sings.)*

JUST PULL IT GENTLY WITH A TWIST,
TAKE HOLD—

(She follows instructions.)

SATAN. *(Sings.)*
—THERE, YOU'VE GOT IT — IT'S DONE!
ENJOY ITS SCENT; WHO CAN RESIST
SO LUSCIOUS A FRUIT AS THIS ONE?
WHY SHOULDN'T YOU EAT THE APPLE?
YOU'VE GOT IT RIGHT THERE IN YOUR HAND!
BITE DEEPLY I SAY, AND TASTE FREEDOM TODAY
FROM THAT STUPID, RESTRICTIVE COMMAND!
NO MORE WILL YOU HAVE TO KOWTOW,
OR DO ONLY WHAT HE WILL ALLOW.
WHY SHOULDN'T YOU EAT THE APPLE?

(She abruptly takes a bite.)

SATAN. *(Sings.)*
YOU SHOULD — AND YOU'RE EATING IT NOW!
(Laughs hideously.)
EVE. *(Looks offstage.)* Oh, dear! Here comes Adam, and — oh my!
— He's stark naked!
SATAN. He doesn't know that. But a bite of the apple will open
his eyes. Go ahead — talk him into it. He'll thank you for it!
EVE. Well — if you really think so...?
SATAN. Would I lie to you?!
ADAM. *(Enters, stops in horror.)* Eve! That apple! What have you
done? Oh, are *you* ever in trouble!
EVE. Aw, Adam, don't be that way. Come on, try a little bite!
ADAM. Are you crazy, woman? God isn't going to like it!
EVE. *(like wives throughout the history of the world)* You don't love
me anymore!
ADAM. Aw! Honey — don't cry — please — I do *so* love you!
Honest, I do!

(Music intros, and:)

EVE. *(Sings.)*
IF YOU LOVE ME, YOU WOULDN'T LET ME FACE THIS
ALL ALONE.
IF YOU LOVE ME, YOU'D HAVE MORE UNDERSTANDING
THAN YOU'VE SHOWN.

ADAM. But Eve—!

EVE. *(Sings.)*
I MAKE ONE MISTAKE AND, BROTHER, DO YOU COMPLAIN!
YOUR HIGH AND MIGHTY ATTITUDE IS GIVING ME A PAIN!
IF YOU LOVE ME,
YOU'D NEVER BE SO CALLOUS OR SO CRUEL.
IF YOU LOVE ME,
YOU WOULDN'T LET ME STAND HERE LIKE A FOOL.
SO BE WHAT YOU SAY AND TRY TO DISPLAY
CONCERN FOR THE WAY I FEEL,
AND CONVINCE ME THAT YOUR LOVE IS REAL!

ADAM. How can you doubt? I've never *looked* at another woman!

(And as she petulantly repeats her song from the start, he joins her and sings.)

ADAM. *(Sings.)*
I LOVE YOU, EVE. YOU MUST BELIEVE
THERE'S NOTHING YOU COULD ASK OF ME I WOULD-
N'T DO.
SAY THE WORD AND I'LL BE THERE.
BE ASSURED I REALLY CARE.
I LOVE YOU, EVE. YOU CAN'T CONCEIVE
OF ALL THE FEELING IN MY HEART I HAVE FOR YOU.
YOU ARE ALL THE MATTERS, ANYWAY.
SO TAKE MY LOVE TODAY!
(At song's finish, he takes apple, takes a bite.)

EVE. There! Isn't it yummy?!

ADAM. *(gaping)* Eve! You're stark naked!

EVE. Well, so are you!

GOD. Adam?

ADAM. Yipe! It's the Lord! Quick, get these leaves on you!

(They duck from view behind hedge.)

GOD. *(in the tone of any loving parent who sees a child with crumbs on his mouth near an emptied cookie jar)* Adam ... where are you?

ADAM. Here, Lord. In the bushes.

GOD. Why are you hiding?

ADAM. Because I'm naked, Lord.

GOD. And who told you you were naked?

ADAM. *(Finally emerges from behind hedge in leafy loincloth.)* Well, it's a funny thing, but — one bite of that fruit, and all at once I started noticing things — things that I never paid much heed to before...

GOD. You are speaking of the fruit that you were forbidden to eat?

ADAM. I'm afraid so, Lord.

GOD. And why did you eat that fruit?

ADAM. The woman! *She* gave me some! The woman *you* put here!

SATAN. That's it! Don't take the blame! Pass the buck!

GOD. Oh, I nearly forgot about you, serpent. Start eating dust!

SATAN. *(Flops flat on his face.)* Wait! Let me out of this body, first! *(Flings serpent-cap offstage, gets to his feet.)*

GOD. Adam, where is the woman?

EVE. *(Emerges, leaf-clad, from behind hedge.)* Here, Lord. But don't put all the blame on me. It wasn't my idea, it was the serpent's.

GOD. You realize, of course, that this means trouble for you?

ADAM. Uh ... what kind of trouble, Lord?

GOD. Oh, things like storms—

(Stage lights flicker, lightning-like; thunder rolls.)

GOD. —and cold—

(Wind sound starts; backdrop fades to black.)

GOD. —and good hard work from now on, for you and all your descendants.

ADAM. Work? What's that?

EVE. I don't like the sound of it.

GOD. And, of course ... death.

ADAM. Death?

GOD. I made you from the dust — and to dust you must return.

SATAN. Now you're talking! This is the end of your creation!

GOD. Oh, no. Not by a long shot. This is just the beginning!

(Stage lights fade slowly during the following.)

GOD. Now, come on, my children. Those silly leaves won't keep you warm. Let me make you some fur garments.

EVE. Why, that's — very nice of you, Lord.

ADAM. I thought you didn't like us anymore.

GOD. How poorly you know me, Adam. If anything, in your new helplessness, I love you more than ever!

BLACKOUT

ACT ONE
Scene Two

In darkness, we hear:

SATAN. God, why don't you just give *up* on people! They'll never do your will, never! Just call it a bad job, and wipe 'em all out!

GOD. If you don't mind, I have other plans.

SATAN. But it's all been such a bust! First Cain kills Abel, then the Tower of Babel! Humanity's name should be mud! But still you go and give warning to Noah, just before the Flood!

GOD. He is a good man. And his wife and children aren't bad, either. When I asked him to build the ark, he started work the same day.

SATAN. You should've let him drown!

GOD. But then who would tell the tale of the Flood to future generations? The Flood was created to serve as a warning to mankind, not an end to mankind.

SATAN. How can you love Noah? All he does is complain!

GOD. I don't mind. After all, I've given him plenty to complain about!

(Stage lighting comes up, and backdrop — interior of the ark — comes up; we see NOAH pacing back and forth, and his WIFE seated in a chair, knitting.)

NOAH. The Lord is good, the Lord is just, the Lord is fair.

WIFE. Noah, can't you pray to yourself?

NOAH. Sometimes I think that's what I *am* doing! I keep praising the Lord, and He never answers! Maybe He's not even there!

WIFE. Don't be silly! He foretold the Flood, didn't He? We'd be awful wet right now if He hadn't!

NOAH. Well — I guess you're right, Wife. He did tell us how to build this ark — and how big to build it — and what to stock it with.... But that was thirty-nine days and nights ago, and I'm getting mighty tired of it!

WIFE. The ark, Noah?

NOAH. What? Oh, no, the ark's not so bad — a little crowded, but not so bad. But there's one thing that is going to drive me bananas!

WIFE. What thing, dear?

NOAH. You've got to be kidding! Think, Woman! What's small and wet and drops down from the skies and *keeps* dropping down from the skies, and drums and splashes and dribbles and thumps, day after day after day?

WIFE. Oh. That.

NOAH. Oh, yes! Precisely that! *(Music intros, and he sings.)*
RAIN! RAIN! THIS PRECIPITATION
FOR SUCH A DURATION
IS STARTING TO DRIVE ME INSANE!

WIFE. *(Still knitting, nods, and sings.)*
RAIN! RAIN! IT'S VERY APPALLING
THE WAY IT KEEPS FALLING
AND COVERING UP THE TERRAIN!

NOAH. *(Sings.)*
I'M STUCK ABOARD THIS FLOATING ZOO
AND A PILE OF MANURE IS COLLECTING!

WIFE. *(Sighs, stands, sings.)*
WE'VE JUST FOUND OUT THE KANGAROO
AND THE ELEPHANT BOTH ARE EXPECTING!

NOAH. *(Sings.)*
RAIN! RAIN! NOT EVEN MY FAMILY'S
BEEN ANY HELP TO ME,
THEY SIT AROUND AND COMPLAIN
ABOUT RAIN, RAIN, RAIN!

WIFE. *(Drops knitting on chair, wrings her hands, sings.)*
RAIN! RAIN! THIS INFERNAL MOISTURE'S
MADE NOAH SO BOISTEROUS
LIVING WITH HIM IS A PAIN!

NOAH. *(Sings.)*
RAIN! RAIN! AND ALL OF HER HEADACHES

WHEN WE GO TO BED MAKES
ONE HELLUVA MARITAL STRAIN!

WIFE. *(Sings.)*

IT REALLY IS COMEDIC HOW
EVERYBODY ABOARD ISN'T SPEAKING!

NOAH. *(Sings.)*

THE OCELOT GOT SEASICK, NOW
I'VE DISCOVERED THE ARK'S STARTED LEAKING!

NOAH and WIFE. *(Both sing.)*

RAIN! RAIN! WE'VE HAD IT RIGHT UP TO HERE;
LORD, CAN'T YOU SEE THAT WE'RE ASKING YOU,
PLEASE, TO REFRAIN
FROM SENDING ANOTHER DROP!
OH, PLEASE, WON'T YOU KINDLY STOP
ALL THIS RAIN! RAIN! RAIN!

(At song's end, both widen eyes, listening.)

NOAH. Hey — I think the rain just stopped!

WIFE. How can you be certain?

NOAH. I'll send out a *pigeon!*

WIFE. Don't look at *me!*

NOAH. I mean a *real* one!

WIFE. Oh. And then what?

NOAH. If it doesn't come back, we know there's dry land out there!

WIFE. Or that it drowned.

NOAH. Oh, look on the bright side, Woman! Cheer up! There's a rainbow in the sky!

WIFE. What's a rainbow?

GOD. Something new I just invented. It's a reminder to you, after every rain, that I won't destroy the earth by *flood* again.

NOAH. Oh, thank you, Lord, thank you! No more destruction of the earth! *(Starts to go off, calling:)* Ham! Shem! Japheth! Come up here and see the rainbow!

WIFE. *(Stops him.)* Wait! The Lord didn't say *no* destruction — He just said never again by *flood.*

NOAH. Nonsense! Why, I'm *sure* there won't be any more destruction.

(Stage lights and backdrop start to dim.)

Wife. How can you be so sure?

Noah. Easy. Once mankind hears about the flood, they'll shape up, and there won't be any more *need* to punish them, don't you see?

Wife. I dunno — I have this sneaking suspicion people can be awfully stupid about toeing the line. Why, they might even refuse to *believe* there *was* a flood!

Noah. How could they? There'll be evidence in the very earth for all the coming ages of Man to discover! *No*body could be *that* stupid!

BLACKOUT

ACT ONE
Scene Three

In the darkness, we hear:

SATAN. So mankind has had its warning, has it? Ha! A lot of good that Flood did you! People are just as bad as ever — some even worse than before! Why don't you just give up? Given the choice, people will *never* be loyal to you, not when there are so many nice *evil* things to do instead!

GOD. What they need is a good example — a group of people especially dedicated to me — a group they can see and study, and understand at last the wisdom of following my laws.

SATAN. What group? There's nothing but howling tribes, all over the planet — a couple of cities — and that's about it!

GOD. I can create a new group — make a covenant with them.

SATAN. Nonsense! Why, the best man — by *your* standards — on the entire earth is so old, already, and his wife totally barren, besides, that they'd be lucky if they could found an old folks' home, let alone a God-fearing nation!

GOD. You mean Abram, don't you! *(This is pronounced "ah-BRAHM.")*

SATAN. *(uneasily)* Oh. You — uh — noticed him, huh?

GOD. Of course I noticed him. His light shines before men like a flame.

(Stage lights come up full; backdrop shows the front door of a small cottage; SARAH is dozing in a chair; ABRAHAM [as he'll later be called] is reading from a piece of parchment, frowning unhappily.)

ABRAHAM. I don't like it, Sarah, not at all. My nephew, Lot, could be in a terrible position should the Lord decide to wreak vengeance upon that wicked city in which he dwells.... Sarah?

...Oh, the sweet darling is asleep. I guess Lot *does* write dull letters... *(Rolls up parchment, sticks it into his robe.)*

GOD. Abram!

ABRAHAM. *(Looks upward.)* Who's that?

GOD. I am the Lord.

ABRAHAM. *(Drops to his knees.)* Really? Why — why are you calling *me*, Lord? I do hope this is not my time to go to you — my wife is old — she needs me — she'd have a terrible time without me around — so, if it's all the same to you—

GOD. Be at peace, Abram. You shall not be called for many years hence. I have decided to bless your union with a child.

ABRAHAM. A child? At *my* age? How? My wife Sarah is barren, Lord.

GOD. Nevertheless, she shall conceive and bear you a son.

ABRAHAM. *(Gets to his feet.)* A son? After all these years? Oh, Lord, how can I thank you?

GOD. You shall raise him in my ways. That will be thanks enough, Abram.

SATAN. *(Enters, unnoticed by ABRAHAM.)* That's not fair, Lord! She's too old! Cut out the miracles!

ABRAHAM. Dear Lord, is it all right if I tell Sarah? I mean — she's kind of nervous. Finding out she was pregnant might shake her up. I think she should have fair warning.

GOD. By all means, Abram. Tell your wife.

SATAN. She'll laugh in his face.

GOD. No she won't. Sarah is a good woman.

SATAN. Oh yes she will! I'll *make* her laugh in his face!

ABRAHAM. *(Has moved to SARAH, shakes her.)* Sarah! Sarah, wake up!

SARAH. Abram! What is it? What are you so excited about? Calm down!

ABRAHAM. Calm Down? Sarah, I have just been speaking with the Lord!

SARAH. But you speak with the Lord every day, Abram. Let me return to my nap.

ABRAHAM. You don't understand. This time it's different! This time the Lord spoke back!

SARAH. *(Stands.)* He did? What did He *say?*

ABRAHAM. *(Music intros, and he sings.)*
WE'RE GONNA HAVE A BABY!

(She staggers.)

ABRAHAM. *(Sings.)*
DON'T HAVE A CARDIAC!
WE'RE GONNA HAVE A BABY!
WE'LL CALL HIM I-SA-AC!
I GUARANTEE
YOU'RE GONNA BE
GALUMPHING AROUND FOR JOY!
SO DON'T YOU FRET,
WE'RE GONNA GET
A BABY BOY!
(He will dance happily about the stage, during:)
SATAN. *(From behind SARAH, sings into her ear.)*
YOU'RE TOO OLD TO DO IT, NO MATTER WHAT HE
ASSERTS!
SARAH, YOU WOULD RUE IT! HAVIN' A BABY HURTS!
PREGNANCY'S A HELL OF A SPREE! TAKE A VOW OF
CELIBACY!
TELL HIM "NYET!" AND DON'T BEGET THAT BABY BOY!
SARAH. *(As ABRAHAM takes her hands and dances her about.)*
WHAT WOULD I TELL THE NEIGHBORS?
HOW COULD I EXPLAIN?
GOING INTO LABOR
SO LATE IN LIFE IS A PAIN!
(Pulls free, but brightens as she continues.)
BUT WHAT FUN
TO TELL OF MY SON
TO THE JEALOUS NEIGHBORS I COULD ANNOY!
SO LET'S BEGET
WITHOUT REGRET
OUR BABY BOY!

*(SATAN is furious, and as ABRAHAM again dances her about the stage, he
follows after them and tries his ploy again, all three singing their
individual parts in counterpoint.)*

SATAN. *(finishing his part, as he gloomily goes offstage)* Oy-yoy-yoy-yoy!

SARAH. Stop with the dancing, already! I'll be too tired to make love!

ABRAHAM. Oh, my darling!

(They embrace, and lights fade to black.)

GOD. Well, we're off to a good start.

SATAN. Bah! Of course he's happy! You've *given* him something! But see how much he loves you if you try and take that something away!

GOD. I have confidence in Abram.

SATAN. So why not *test* him a little, then?

GOD. All right. I will. As soon as Isaac grows up.

SATAN. That's too long! Abram will be set in his ways, then. How about while Isaac is still a young boy?

GOD. Very well. Let's see what happens.

(Lights come up full again; SARAH is again dozing in chair; ABRAHAM is reading another parchment; ISAAC — about 10 years old — is trying to read the parchment, too.)

ISAAC. Father, what else does cousin Lot say? His Hebrew is hard to read.

ABRAHAM. Same old thing, my son. The city in which he lives is more wicked than ever. He really should clear out of there, and soon. The hand of the Lord will not be stayed forever.

ISAAC. But what can the Lord do? He promised no more floods.

ABRAHAM. He'll think of something. His imagination is limitless, son.

ISAAC. Father, how do you know so much about God?

ABRAHAM. It's easy to know him. His presence can be detected in all phases of creation — order and system don't just happen — they must be imposed from without. The movements of the stars in the heavens, the parade of season following season, day following night, a blossom producing a fruit, containing a seed, which will produce a tree, which will in its turn produce a blossom—

ISAAC. *(Boy-like, is already tiring of the conversation.)* Fruit! That reminds me, Father — the fig tree at the end of the yard is sagging with the weight of its fruit. Might I go and pick some?

ABRAHAM. The fruit hangs high — you'll need some help. Sarah—?

SARAH. *(Wakens.)* Yes, my husband?

ABRAHAM. Our son wants some figs. Will you help him get some?

SARAH. Oh, of course. Come along, Isaac — and bring that chair — the fruit hangs very high.

(They exit with chair.)

GOD. Abram!
ABRAHAM. Yes, Lord?

(Backdrop will fade completely during dialogue.)

GOD. I would like you to do something for me.

ABRAHAM. You have but to name it, Lord, and if it is within my power, it shall be done.

GOD. Very well. I want you to go up to the mountain and offer sacrifice to me.

ABRAHAM. I shall depart at once, Lord.

GOD. Take your son, Isaac, with you.

ABRAHAM. Oh, certainly, Lord! Isaac! Isaac, come here! But Lord, there are no animals atop the mountain — what shall be the sacrifice?

GOD. Your son, Isaac, shall be the sacrifice.

(ABRAHAM is staggered, but does not reply.)

GOD. Well, Abram? Have you nothing to say? No questions to ask?

ABRAHAM. *(quietly)* The Lord giveth, and the Lord taketh away.

ISAAC. *(Rushes onstage.)* You called me, Father?

ABRAHAM. Yes, my son. I want you to come with me to the top of the mountain. There I must offer sacrifice to the Lord.

ISAAC. Oh, good! Let me just go and tell Mother—

ABRAHAM. Time enough to tell her later, when I return.

ISAAC. When *we* return, you mean.

ABRAHAM. *(heartbroken)* Do not quibble, son. Come along, now.

(They will "walk" as backdrop lights up with rocky terrain, and ABRAHAM starts to sing.)

ABRAHAM. *(Sings.)*
WE'RE GOIN' UP TO THE MOUNTAIN!

ISAAC. *(Happily moving along with him, overlap-sings.)*
GOIN' UP TO THE MOUNTAIN!

ABRAHAM. *(Sings.)*
TO MAKE A SACRIFICE!

ISAAC. *(Sings.)*
MAKE A SACRIFICE!

ABRAHAM. *(Sings.)*
WE'RE GOIN' UP TO THE MOUNTAIN!
UP UNTIL THE COMIN' DOWN!

ISAAC. *(Sings.)*
HARD GOIN' UP, BUT STILL, THE COMIN' DOWN IS NICE!

ABRAHAM. *(His heartbreak showing in his voice, sings.)*
THE COMIN' DOWN! OH, LORD! CAN I DO IT?!

ISAAC. *(Sings.)*
COMIN' DOWN TOGETHER! TOGETHER HAND-IN-HAND!

ABRAHAM. *(Sings.)*
MY HAND WAS MADE TO SERVE THE LORD,
BUT HOW CAN I SERVE HIM WITH A BROKEN HEART?

ISAAC. *(Sings.)*
WE'LL SERVE THE LORD, THEN START
TOGETHER DOWN THE MOUNTAIN TO DEPART!

(Spoken over continuing music:) Father, are there very many animals there?

ABRAHAM. Where?

ISAAC. Up on the mountain.

ABRAHAM. I don't follow you.

ISAAC. Father, how can you not know what I mean? We need an animal!

ABRAHAM. Oh, you mean something for the sacrifice!

ISAAC. Yes, of course!

ABRAHAM. Well, son, don't worry! The Lord will provide!

ISAAC. Yes, I guess you're right! He always comes through when we need Him, doesn't He!

ABRAHAM. Son, you talk too much. Come along now... *(Sings.)*

UP TO THE MOUNTAIN!

ISAAC. *(Sings.)*

GONNA GO UP TO THE MOUNTAIN!

ABRAHAM. *(Sings.)*

WE MUST DO HIS WILL!
THE LORD OUR GOD IN HIS WISDOM
HAS DECREED THE VICTIM TO KILL!

ISAAC. *(Sings.)*

GOD IN HIS WISDOM WILL PROVIDE
THE VICTIM WE MUST KILL!
I WONDER WHAT IT'LL BE?

ABRAHAM. *(Sings.)*

OH, LORD MY GOD, WILL YOU BESTOW NOW
THE COURAGE TO MY HAND,
AS YOUR STERN COMMAND I NOW FULFILL!

ISAAC. *(Sings.)*

WHAT WILL WE SEE THERE UP ON THE MOUNTAIN
WHERE THE CHOSEN VICTIM'S BLOOD WE'VE VOWED
TO SPILL!

(ABRAHAM stops, draws his knife, takes ISAAC by the arm; music continues under the following dialogue.)

ISAAC. Father, that knife! What does it mean?

ABRAHAM. *You* are the sacrifice, Isaac, my son!

ISAAC. But Father—!

ABRAHAM. It's the will of the Lord! We must not question His reasons!

ISAAC. Oh, but surely—!

ABRAHAM. *(Sings.)*
I'LL TRY TO BE SWIFT, MY SON!

ISAAC. Father, please—! Oh, please—! Dear Father—!

ABRAHAM. *(Sings.)*
THE WILL OF THE LORD MUST BE DONE,
AND I AM THE SERVANT OF THE LORD—!
(He raises his knife.)

GOD. *(over music)* Do not harm the boy! You have done my will! There is a ram in the bushes up yonder! Use that! And my blessings on you forever!

ABRAHAM. *(Lowers and re-sheathes the knife, speaks from the heart.)* Thank you, Lord!

ISAAC. *(Sings.)*
WE'RE GOIN' UP TO THE MOUNTAIN!

(As they start walking again.)

ABRAHAM. (Sings.)
UP TO THE MOUNTAIN!

ISAAC. *(Sings.)*
TO SATISFY THE LORD!

ABRAHAM. *(Sings.)*
SATISFY THE LORD!

ISAAC. *(Sings.)*
WE DON'T MIND CLIMBING THE MOUNTAIN
WITH OUR HAPPINESS RESTORED!

ABRAHAM. *(Sings.)*
CLIMBING UP THERE WITH OUR HAPPINESS RESTORED!

ABRAHAM and ISAAC. *(Both sing.)*
WE'LL BE TOGETHER, TOGETHER HAND-IN-HAND
AS WE PLANNED! WE'RE GOIN' UP TO THE MOUNTAIN!

ISAAC. *(Sings.)*
WITHOUT A WORRY!

ABRAHAM and ISAAC. *(Both sing.)*
UP TO THE MOUNTAIN!

Isaac. *(Sings.)*
WE'D BETTER HURRY!
Abraham and Isaac. *(Will cease walk-in-place and exit, on singing:)*
UP THERE TO PRAISE THE LORD!

(Stage lights and backdrop will start to fade, during the following.)

God. What a marvelous man! I'm proud to have created him! After he sacrifices the ram, I shall change his name from Abram to Abraham. He shall found a great people, a people numerous as the stars of the sky, and they shall be my people alone. Imagine the devotion of that man — he was willing to sacrifice his only son for me! ... Now, I guess, I *owe* him one!

God #2. Father, your will is my will.

God. Son — I love you very much.

God #2. I know, Father.

God. Yet no one shall say that the Lord demands more of his people than he, himself, would be willing to do.

God #2. I will make certain that no one will be able to truthfully say otherwise.

God. It won't be easy, my son.

God #2. Love is never easy.

BLACKOUT

ACT ONE
Scene Four

Stage lights and backdrop — a rocky terrain — come up, and we see SATAN, center stage, looking off right.

SATAN. What's going on over there? Who are all these people approaching?

GOD. Abraham has given warning to his nephew, Lot. Those are Lot and his wife, their family and friends, fleeing the city of Sodom before I destroy it and destroy Gomorrah, its sister city. The wickedness of those cities is an abomination in my face.

SATAN. A fine loving God you are!

GOD. They have had every warning — by prophets, by angelic messengers, by the words of the Scriptures. Yet they persist in their evil. Their destruction shall be as a warning to future generations.

SATAN. And what do Lot and his people do? Stand here and cheer? Gloat in their sanctimonious righteousness?

(LOT, his WIFE, and OTHERS will enter now.)

GOD. No, that would be a temptation to pride. They shall not view the destruction. *(Calls.)* Lot!

(LOT and the OTHERS with him stop.)

LOT. Yes, Lord?

GOD. Are these all the good people that could be found in the cities?

LOT. I fear so, Lord. Even though my uncle, Abraham, convinced you to spare the cities if he could find so much as ten just men therein. These are all he did find — this handful of men and women.

GOD. So be it. Then hear my command. You and your family and your friends shall now march away from the cities, and under no circumstances are you to look back upon them, no matter what you hear behind you! Is that understood? Those who look shall become pillars of salt!

LOT. Yes, Lord. We all understand. Come on, everybody!

WIFE. What? No backward look? To the city where we dwelt so many years? Never more to look again upon those towering gates, upon the streets where I did my marketing, upon the beautiful buildings?

LOT. The Lord has commanded, Woman, and we must obey! Come along, now!

WIFE. But darling — what harm is there in but a single glance?

LOT. To disobey the Lord is harm enough to befall anyone. Think no longer of our past lives there. We go to a new and better life.

WIFE. But, Husband, I pray you. Just one final look of farewell?

LOT. The Lord has spoken, and we must obey! Come along, everybody!

(All will "walk" away from cities as he sings.)

LOT. *(Sings.)*
DON'T LOOK BACK, IT'S ALL BEHIND US NOW!
DON'T LOOK BACK, FOR GOD REMINDS US NOW:
WE SHOULD BE LOOKING AHEAD
TO OUR DESTINATION INSTEAD!
DON'T LOOK BACK, KEEP MOVIN' ON, I SAY!
IT'S ALL RACK AND RUIN ANYWAY!

(Intense light begins to glow offstage behind them.)

LOT. *(Sings.)*
SODOM, I TRUST, IS AFLAME;
GOMORRAH WOULD JUST BE THE SAME!

*(As they "walk," WIFE straggles until she is at rear of moving group, with
      SATAN just behind her.)*

Lot. *(Sings.)*
DON'T YOU SEE? YOUR CURIOSITY
COULD REALLY BE A TERRIBLE FAULT!
IF YOU DO, THE LORD HAS PROMISED YOU
WILL TURN INTO A PILLAR OF SALT!
DON'T LOOK BACK, IT'S ALMOST OUT OF SIGHT!
KEEP ON TRACK AND MAKE IT THROUGH THE NIGHT.

(Backdrop will fade to total black over next lines.)

Lot. *(Sings.)*
EVEN THOUGH THINGS MIGHT LOOK BLACK,
WE MUST MAINTAIN OUR NEW TACK,
AND DON'T LOOK BACK!
Satan. *(As music continues, wheedles insistently at WIFE, singing.)*
WHERE'S THE HARM? TAKE A PEEK,
BE A CLEVER LITTLE SNEAK!
TAKE A PEEK, GET A GLOM,
THEN GO ON WITHOUT A QUALM!
WHERE'S THE HARM IN BEING A LITTLE OBSERVANT,
AND NOBODY'S SERVANT?
GET A GLOM, HAVE A LOOK
WHILE THE OTHERS CROSS THE BROOK!
HAVE A LOOK, JUST A PEEP,
FOR A MEMORY TO KEEP!
FIND THE FACTS AND REAP THE REWARDS OF YOUR
LABORS,
ONE UP ON YOUR NEIGHBORS!
HURRY UP AND DO IT! TIME IS FADING FAST!
DON'T LET YOUR FOOTSTEPS ROAM!
TURN AROUND AND VIEW IT! THIS MAY BE THE LAST
SIGHT OF YOUR HOME, SWEET HOME!
JUST A PEEP! FLICK AN EYE!
YOU JUST WANNA SAY GOODBYE!
FLICK AN EYE! WHERE'S THE HARM?

HAVE NO FEELINGS OF ALARM!
GOD SAID IT WAS WRONG,
BUT THAT'S JUST HIS OLD SONG AND DANCE—
TAKE A CHANCE!

(Now LOT — along with all others except WIFE, if desired — starts repeating his song while SATAN repeats his own song, with a slight lyric-variation toward the end.)

    Lot [and Others. (optional)] *(Sings.)*
DON'T TEMPT FATE, JUST TRY TO CONCENTRATE
ON WHAT NEW LIFE AWAITS US TODAY!
JUST KEEP GOING, PUT YOUR FAITH IN KNOWING
THAT THE LORD IS SHOWING THE WAY!
    Satan. *(Sings.)*
WHEN GOD SAID TO TAKE IN THE SCENE WAS FORBID-
DEN,
HE WAS JUST KIDDIN' AND HE WON'T FIND FAULT!
COME TO A HALT!

WIFE stops, and as she turns to look.)

    Satan. *(Sings.)*
ATTA GIRL!

(and as she turns into a pillar of salt.)

    Satan. *(Sings.)*
PASS THE SALT!

(Note: The transformation is simple: If she is wearing pastel shades of blue, green and white, and the intense light from the wings is bright blue, and the stage lights go to black, the blue will "wash out" all the other colors in her face and clothing [if she is a blonde, the hair will change similarily] and as she freezes in position, eyes wide and mouth agape, it will seem as if she has literally changed substance before our eyes. She need only hold this stance long enough for others and LOT to walk offstage the way they were headed.)

BLACKOUT

ACT ONE
Scene Five

*Interior of rustic kitchen appears on backdrop as stage lights come up;
JACOB stands center stage, stirring something in a pot whose handle
he holds in one hand, spoon in the other; ESAU enters from left.*

Esau. Boy, am I ever pooped, Jacob. Say, what's in that pot?

Jacob. Pottage.

Esau. Sure smells good.

Jacob. I hope so. It may be Father's final meal.

Esau. What are you saying?

Jacob. Esau, our father, Isaac, old and blind, lies dying in his
tent. I thought some good food might cheer him up a bit.

Esau. Can I have what's left over?

Jacob. I only made enough for one.

Esau. Aw, come on, Jacob! I've been out hunting all night and
most of the morning — couldn't even catch a field mouse — I'm
hungry enough to eat a boiled sandal!

Jacob. I could make you some more — it'll only take an
hour or so.

Esau. I could starve to death by then! Come on, let me have the
pottage. I'll give you anything you ask for it.

Jacob. Such as what? Your hunting bow? Your hunting knife?
Your hunting dogs? Esau, I don't like hunting.

Esau. I'll give you the carcass of the next deer I catch. Deer hide
makes great sandals.

Jacob. Fair enough. Give me the hide, and I'll give you the
pottage.

Esau. Can't I have it on credit?

Jacob. Esau, the pottage is getting cold. I'd better take it to
our father.

Esau. No, wait! There must be *something* of mine you'll take
for it!

JACOB. *(as if casually)* Well — let me see — how about your birthright?

SATAN. *(Pops in from right, landing in a crouch.)* Hey, a con game! Brother against brother! If there's one thing I love, it's a good scam!

ESAU. My birthright? But that belongs to the firstborn son. I was the firstborn son. How can I turn it over to you?

JACOB. Just say it's mine, and I'll take care of the rest.

ESAU. Well ... I don't know—

JACOB. Okay, I'll just take this pottage to Father—

ESAU. No! Wait! Look, this is a serious decision, and — Oh, all right, give me the pottage!

JACOB. Not so fast! Have we got a deal?

ESAU. Yes, yes, it's a deal! Now hand it over! *(Takes pot and spoon, almost eats, then sees JACOB is leaving.)* Where are *you* off to so fast?

JACOB. To get our father's blessing as the first born.

ESAU. Jacob, *he* won't give it to *you*! Pottage or no pottage, our father, Isaac, will still reserve his blessing for *me*.

JACOB. Don't be so sure. Our mother, Rebecca, and I figured out a way to fool him. I'll tie furs around my arms so they feel as hairy as yours, and speak in a gruff voice like yours. I'll pull it off somehow.

ESAU. What a rotten trick on a dying man! *(Exits right, eating pottage.)*

JACOB. Yes, I guess it is. But Mother doesn't seem to mind.

ESAU. *(off)* She always *did* like you better! You with your soft hands and quiet ways and skinny frame!

JACOB. *(starting off left)* Is it *my* fault Mother's not into macho?! Hey, Mom! The fix is in! *(Exits.)*

SATAN. Whee! What a nice rotten turnabout for God's plans! The grandson of Abraham, cheating his blind father, finagling his way into the descendancy of the Chosen People!

GOD. Everything's going according to plan.

SATAN. What? You *wanted* Jacob next in line?

GOD. My people shall be as a family. Esau isn't much interested in family life. His life lies in the woods and fields. My people shall descend from a lover of home and hearthside. Jacob shall father twelve sons, and I shall change his name to Israel, and his sons shall each father one of the tribes of Israel.

SATAN. Name-changes! Always name-changes! How can anybody tell who's who?!

GOD. *I* know who is who, and what they are about. That is all that matters.

(Stage lights and backdrop start to dim.)

SATAN. It's not fair! You're playing with loaded dice! No matter what goes wrong, no matter how much I interfere, things always end up going *your* way!

GOD. Creation is like a garden. I simply keep weeding out the imperfect to allow for the growth of the better plants. Jacob, even though attaining his position by a trick, will be the better patriarch for my people.

SATAN. I'll lure the twelve tribes away from you! I'll make them turn against you! Then what will you do?

(It is almost totally dark, now.)

GOD. I shall let them fall into enslavement by the Egyptians. Then, when they have learned to look only to me for comfort, I shall send a man named Moses to lead them to freedom.

SATAN. No matter! I shall turn them against him, as well!

GOD. But for how long, Satan? For how long?

BLACKOUT

ACT ONE
Scene Six

Stage lights and backdrop — sky and craggy peaks — come up fast; Israelites and SATAN — who wears a headcloth "disguise" in their midst — are standing about, one or two seated on the ground.

WOMAN. I'm getting awfully tired of just hanging around.

MAN. Me, too! I thought we were on the way to the Promised Land!

WOMAN #2. Personally, I don't think there *is* any Promised Land!

MAN #2. We were better off back in Egypt!

SATAN. It's all the fault of Moses! You should leave without him!

WOMAN #3. How long's he been gone, anyhow?

MAN #3. I make it forty days!

WOMAN #4. Forty days! And I thought this was just a rest stop!

MAN. Yeah. I've had about all the rest I can use!

WOMAN #5. Now, wait. Moses said something about getting the laws of God.

MAN #2. That takes forty days?!

WOMAN #3. There must be an awful lot of them!

MAN #3. Even if he brings them — how are we going to *remember* them all?!

SATAN. Even if you could — who does God think he is, ordering people around?! And what are laws, anyway? A few pen-scratches on a piece of parchment!

WOMAN. Yeah! They'll crumble in a year's time!

MAN. We were fools to follow Moses out into the desert!

WOMAN #2. It beats being enslaved!

MAN #2. But not by much!

WOMAN #3. I thought the laws would be carved into stone? You know, to be sort of *permanent* guidelines for us.

MAN #3. Even if they are, I'm getting mighty tired of being pushed around!

SATAN. We *all* are! Who *needs* Moses?!

OTHERS. Yeah, who *needs* him?!

SATAN. Who *needs* this sun-scorched desert life?!

OTHERS. Yeah, who *needs* it?!

SATAN. And as for those silly laws, carven into solid stone or not— *(Music intros, and he sings.)*

WHY SHOULD YOU OBEY THE COMMANDMENTS?
A COUPLE OF HUNKS OF STONE!
I JUST CAN'T CONCEIVE
THAT YOU'D BE SO NAIVE;
TELL OLD MOSES TO LEAVE YOU ALONE!

OTHERS. Yeah!

SATAN. *(Sings.)*

WHY SHOULD YOU OBEY THE COMMANDMENTS?
A BUNCH OF RESTRICTIVE RULES!
GREAT HEAVENS ABOVE!
DON'T YOU KNOW THAT HE'D LOVE
TO MAKE ALL OF YOU GROVEL LIKE FOOLS?

OTHERS. No way!

SATAN. *(Sings.)*

I REALLY AM CONVINCED THAT YOUR
INVISIBLE GOD IS A LAUGH!
YOU NEED A NEW GOD TO ADORE;
I'VE GOT IT! A SOLID GOLD CALF!

OTHERS. Now you're talking!

SATAN. *(Sings.)*

WHY SHOULD YOU OBEY THE COMMANDMENTS?
DON'T GIVE IN TO ANYONE.
INSTEAD, WHY DON'T YOU
HAVE AN ORGY OR TWO,
'CAUSE YOU'RE LONG OVERDUE FOR SOME FUN?

OTHERS. Right on!

SATAN. *(Sings.)*

DON'T BE LIKE SOME SHEEP IN A FOLD

AND DO EV'RY DUMB THING THAT YOU'RE TOLD!
I'LL GIVE YOU A NEW RELIGION—
BUT FIRST, GIVE ME ALL OF YOUR GOLD!
(Laughs hideously.)

(Israelites cheer, and start handing him rings and other jewelry.)

SATAN. *(He carries jewelry off left, speaking as he exits.)* I'll take care of the calf — you get the *orgy* going!
WOMAN. *(Calls after him.)* I've never attended an orgy before!
MAN. Me, neither! How do we go about it?
SATAN. *(off)* It's easy! Just take normal conduct and carry it to extremes! The secret of a successful orgy is — nothing exceeds like excess!
OTHERS. Right! *(Music intros, and they sing.)*
LEER A LITTLE, SNEER A LITTLE,
EAT TILL YOU DISGORGE!
WE'RE AT AN ORGY THAT'LL KNOCK OUR SOCKS OFF!
GONNA THROW A FIT, ALTHOUGH OUR
COMMON SENSE DISCLOSES MAYBE MOSE IS
GONNA KNOCK OUR BLOCKS OFF!
HAVE A YEN! INDULGE IN ANY MOOD YOU CRAVE! YOUR
OPTIONS NEVER STOP! IT'S TIME FOR LEWD BEHAVIOR!
TIME HAS COME TO START NEUROTIC RAVES AND
RANTS,
SO GRAB YOURSELF A PARTNER FOR A PAGAN
DANCE—!
(Music goes crazy, and they do a dance of wild abandon.)

*(As they dance, SATAN re-enters with golden calf, which he sets upstage
     center.)*

OTHERS. *(They finish dance and sing, just a little breathlessly.)*
GO EASY NOW AND TAKE A REST!
THIS QUEASY FEELING IN MY CHEST
IS MAKIN' IT JUST A BIT HARD TO LAUGH,
AND FROLIC AND ROLLICK FOR THIS STUPID CALF!

(Optionally, SATAN can join singers here.)

OTHERS. *(Sing.)*
BUT LIVES OF DARK DEBAUCHERY
CONTRIVE A FEARSOME LITTLE FEE!
WE CANNOT HALT OUR ASSAULT OF DEGEN—
ERATE ACTS OR RELAX! IT'S TIME TO DANCE AGAIN!
(Music goes even crazier as they dance again; this time, the dancing — with weary motions — continues even as they gaspingly [minus SATAN, if he joined in last time] sing onwards.)
WE'RE SAGGIN' NOW!
WE'RE DRAGGIN' NOW!
UNFLAGGIN' MISCONDUCT DISENCHANTS!
IT'S VILLAINOUS!
IT'S KILLIN' US!
BUT STILL WE MUST GO ON WITH THE DANCE!
(Music and dance go berserk, now, with lurches, leaps and staggers rushing toward a cacaphonous climax.)

*(MOSES — the twin tablets in his arms — enters from right and stops
      in consternation.)*

SATAN. *(Sees MOSES, grabs the calf, and exits left, fast.)* Curses! I came so near...!
OTHERS. *(falling prone with relief at MOSES' feet)* Moses! Thank God you're here!
MOSES. Aren't you all ashamed of yourselves!
OTHERS. We certainly are!
MOSES. Well, at least you've learned that sin's not all it's cracked up to be!
OTHERS. That's for darn sure!

(Lights start to fade fast.)

MOSES. Well, get up! We've still got a long way to march!

(as others start to get wearily to their feet:)

BLACKOUT

(Note: In this scene, MAN #3 is played by player who does voice of GOD, since there is no voice of GOD in this scene.)

ACT ONE
Scene Seven

In total darkness, we hear:

SATAN. Well, now, things are looking up at last! I conned Moses into doubting you! Imagine, after ten plagues, the parting of the Red Sea, the carving of the Commandments before his very eyes, manna from heaven, and giving Miriam leprosy when she tried to take over the group, I got him to smack that rock a *second* time to get them water in the desert! They'll never get to the Promised Land, now!

GOD. Of course they will. All except Moses. But I let him see it from afar, didn't I?

SATAN. Sure. Big deal. Forty years of wandering, and no payoff!

GOD. Moses didn't seem to mind. He accepted my decision quite amiably.

SATAN. He's an idiot! *Anyone* who follows your laws is an idiot!

GOD. Moses is quite contented, thank you.

SATAN. Well, your plan is *still* up the creek! Your precious Israelites can't settle into their new homes because of the people in Jericho! They won't *let* the newcomers settle! You've lost! Admit it!

GOD. I never lose.

SATAN. Oh? Then what about the walled city that now stands in their way? A city of people who refuse to share the land with the Israelites? Those walls are sky-high and forty feet thick! What do you expect the Israelites to do — huff and puff and *blow* the walls down?

GOD. You'd be surprised, Satan. You'd be surprised.

(Stage lights and backdrop — a towering expanse of stone wall — come up; Israelites, JOSHUA and SATAN stand before it, their backs to us, looking upward; each will turn downstage, and remain facing downstage, as each speaks his or her line of dialogue.)

MAN. Well, this is the end of the line!

WOMAN. All this way for nothing!

WOMAN #2. What'll we do now?

MAN #2. We can't take on a city that big!

WOMAN #3. You can hardly see the *top* of that wall!

WOMAN #4. It's certainly too high to climb!

WOMAN #5. Even if we tried, they'd drop rocks on us!

SATAN. Why don't you give up, split up the group, and everybody go their separate ways?

JOSHUA. Now, hold on! The Lord God has brought us *this* far! Surely He won't abandon us now!

SATAN. God, God, God! Is that all you know, Joshua?!

OTHERS. Yeah, is that all you know?!

JOSHUA. God is all that's *worth* knowing! *(Calls heavenward.)* Lord! Lord, what's our next move?

GOD. Joshua, what do you have slung from the sash of your tunic?

JOSHUA. Where? Oh, you mean my trumpet, Lord? The one I use to call the people together?

GOD. Exactly. And what can call together can also send apart.

JOSHUA. I — I suppose so, Lord. What precisely are you getting at? You want me to send the people off in all directions?

GOD. No. I want you to send the stones of the walls of Jericho off in all directions.

JOSHUA. Would they answer to my trumpet?

GOD. Don't the people answer to it?

JOSHUA. Well, yes, Lord — but they are your obedient creatures.

GOD. Joshua, I created the entire universe. Everything *in* it is my obedient creature — including the stones in those walls.

JOSHUA. Oh. I never thought of that, Lord. I'll do it!

GOD. The other men have trumpets — let's make this a community effort.

JOSHUA. You've got a deal, Lord! People! People of Israel! Listen to me!

SATAN. *Now* what?!

JOSHUA. I have just heard from the Lord—

SATAN. That's what *you* say!

JOSHUA. Do you want to know how to breach these walls or don't you?

OTHERS. You mean there's a way?

SATAN. Don't listen to him!

OTHERS. But he says there's a way!

JOSHUA. And there *is* a way! Men of Israel, lift up your trumpets!

(They do so.)

MEN. Now what?

JOSHUA. We are going to blow those trumpets, and the stones will heed our call, and the walls will come tumbling down!

SATAN. That's the silliest thing I ever heard in my life!

OTHERS. It's ridiculous!

JOSHUA. After all God has done for you, don't you owe it to Him to at least *try*?

SATAN. You'll all look like *idiots* if you *do*.

OTHERS. We will?

SATAN. Of course you will! Consider the situation! *(Music intros, and he sings.)*

LOOK AT THAT WALL! APPALLINGLY TALL!
NO POWER ON EARTH COULD MAKE IT FALL!
YOU'D BETTER MOVE ON AND WEARILY WANDER
THROUGH THE DESERT SOME MORE!
THAT WALL IS SO HIGH! IT TOUCHES THE SKY!
YOU'D BETTER GIVE UP AND PASS ON BY!
NO TINY BRASS BAND'D MAKE IT STOP STANDIN'
JUST AS TALL AS BEFORE!

(Men [except JOSHUA] and women join SATAN in singing the foregoing through a second time.)

MEN, WOMEN & JOSHUA. *(Sing.)*
BUT STILL, WE OWE IT TO GOD TO BLOW IT,
IF JUST TO SHOW THAT WE GIVE A HOOT!
    SATAN. *(spoken)* Oh, no!
    OTHERS. *(Sing.)*
ITWOULDN'T SHAME US! GOD COULDN'T BLAME US
IF NOTHING CAME OF OUR ROOT-A-TOOT!
    SATAN. Don't blow!

(But already, enthusiastically, the others start.)

    WOMEN. *(Sing.)*
BLOW THAT TRUMPET, BLOW!
    MEN. *(Sing.)*
BLOW UNTIL YOUR EYES POP OUT!
    WOMEN. *(Sing.)*
BLOW THAT TRUMPET, BLOW!
    MEN. *(Sing.)*
BLOW UNTIL YOUR FACE TURNS BLUE!
    WOMEN. *(Sing.)*
BLOW THAT TRUMPET, BLOW!
    MEN. *(Sing.)*
BLOW AND GIVE A MIGHTY SHOUT!
    WOMEN. *(Sing.)*
SHOUT AND BELT IT OUT FROM HEAD TO TOE!
DO LET GO AND—
    MEN. *(Sing.)*
THAT'S WHAT GOD TOLD US TO DO! LET GO AND—
    WOMEN. *(Sing.)*
BLOW THAT TRUMPET, BLOW!
    MEN. *(Sing.)*
BLOW UNTIL YOUR LIPS GIVE WAY!
    WOMEN. *(Sing.)*
BLOW THAT TRUMPET, BLOW!
    MEN. *(Sing.)*
HOLD THE NOTE AND DON'T LET GO!
    WOMEN. *(Sing.)*
BLOW THAT TRUMPET, BLOW!

MEN. *(Sing.)*
BLOW LIKE IT'S THE JUDGEMENT DAY!
WOMEN. *(Sing.)*
HEY, GO ON AND BLOW!
MEN. *(Sing.)*
TAKE YOUR CORNET—
WOMEN. *(Sing.)*
BLOW!
MEN. *(Sing.)*
GET READY, SET—
WOMEN. *(Sing.)*
BLOW!
MEN. *(Sing.)*
BREATHE IN AND LET GO!
WOMEN. *(Sing.)*
WE WANT YOU TO BLOW!
MEN. *(Sing.)*
WHAT'S SLOWIN' YOU?
WOMEN. *(Sing.)*
BLOW!
MEN. *(Sing.)*
WHAT'S THROWIN' YOU?
WOMEN. *(Sing.)*
BLOW!
MEN. *(Sing.)*
WE'RE GOIN' TO SHOW—
WOMEN. *(Sing.)*
—YOU HOW! GO—
MEN and WOMEN. *(Sing.)*
RON-TATA-TA-TA-*TA*! RON-TATA-TA-TA-*TA*!
RON-TATA-TA-TA! *RON*-TATA-TA-TA!
RON-TATA-TA-TA! *RON*-TATA-TA-TA!
BLOW THAT TRUMPET! BLOW THAT TRUMPET!

(All give mighty shout, over which we hear trumpet-blast)

MEN and WOMEN. *Aaaaah!*

(Walls topple [i.e.: acetate-painting slides off lightbox in upstage direction, causing projected image to slide downward on backdrop]; in ensuing silence:)

SATAN. Oh, hell, they *blew* it! ... And *I* blew it! *(He shuffles glumly off, stage left, during:)*
OTHERS. *(Sing, joyfully.)*
ALLELUIA! ALLELUIA! ALLELUIA! ALLELUIA!
(As they sustain final triumphant note—)

The Curtain Falls

END OF ACT ONE

ACT TWO
Scene One

While final chord of Entr'Acte is fading, stage lights and backdrop — the silken interior of a very beautiful tent — come up full; DELILAH is lounging on a chaise, a HANDMAIDEN fanning her, she seems pouty and upset.)

HANDMAIDEN. Is it not a beautiful day, Mistress Delilah?

DELILAH. It's *always* beautiful in the valley. Sun, sun, sun! And this lousy heat!

HANDMAIDEN. Shall I bring you a goblet of chilled wine?

DELILAH. Of course not! That wine is loaded with knockout drops!

HANDMAIDEN. Again? Mistress, why do you bother? It never seems to have any effect upon Samson.

DELILAH. That's because I haven't *given* him any yet! First I have to learn the secret of his strength. *Then* he gets the mickey!

HANDMAIDEN. Oh, mistress, why do you not give it up? He will never tell you his secret. He only pretends to weaken to your charms.

DELILAH. I *can't* give it up! I can't even afford the rental for this tent — not to mention your salary — if I don't get paid off by the Philistines. And if I don't get that secret — they don't pay off!

HANDMAIDEN. Maybe you're using the wrong approach.

DELILAH. What's left? I've asked politely — I've fallen on my knees and begged — I've coaxed, cajoled and wheedled—! You just can't play twenty questions with a clam!

HANDMAIDEN. I have heard, mistress, that music hath charms to soothe the savage breast. Have you tried singing to him? His breast is about the savagest I've ever seen.

DELILAH. Singing—? Singing... Singing! Why not! It's worth a try! *(Sits up, hearkening.)* I hear him approaching! Stop that fanning and get out of here — but don't go further than the wine cooler — and when I call, come running!

(HANDMAIDEN bows, hurries off left just as SAMSON comes striding manfully on from right.)

SAMSON. Delilah! My tender little desert love!

DELILAH. *(Gets up from chaise.)* You don't know the *meaning* of the word love! To love is to trust — and to trust is to confide — we've been lovers for a week, now, and I don't even know your sandal-size!

SAMSON. *(Clasps her to him.)* Ah, but the essence of abiding love is mystery! So long as there are secrets to be learned from me, you will not grow bored with my companionship!

DELILAH. But *all* I want to know is the secret of your invincibility! Don't you trust me?

SAMSON. Now, be logical. If I told you, you'd stop wheedling — and you have the neatest wheedle in the Valley of Sorech!

DELILAH. Aw, come on, be a sport! *(Music intros, and she sings.)*
SAMSON, DEAR, SIT RIGHT HERE,
(Seats him on chaise, sits on his lap.)
TELL ME HOW YOU GET YOUR AWESOME POWER!
CLEAR THE AIR! DON'T YOU DARE
KEEP ME IN THE DARK ANOTHER HOUR!
(Cuddles amorously.)
I'LL MAKE IT WELL WORTH YOUR WHILE,
SAY THE WORD AND DELILAH IS YOURS IF YOU WANT
HER TO BE!
THAT'S MY DEAL, SO REVEAL
WHAT I'M ASKING; WON'T YOU PLEASE APPEASE
MY CURIOSITY!

(Music goes into second intro, during:)

SAMSON. What do you need to know that for?

DELILAH. *(exactly like EVE)* You don't love me anymore!

SAMSON. *(a sinking ship)* Aw, honey, of course I do! I can't stand it when you're blue! *(Sings.)*

WHAT D'YA THINK'S SUPPLYIN'
POWER TO THE LION?
IT'S HIS MANE!
THERE'S AN ALLEGORY
TO MY CROWNING GLORY—
I'LL EXPLAIN:
LIKE THE LION,
THERE'S NO DENYIN'
THERE'S STRENGTH
IN THE LENGTH
OF THE HAIR ON MY BEAN.
IT SHOULD NEVER BE CUT—
THAT'S MY LITTLE SECRET—
NOW YOU KNOW WHAT I MEAN!

(as music re-intros)

DELILAH. *(Leaps from his lap.)* You told me! I'm so pleased! I want to celebrate! *(Calls.)* Handmaiden! Bring wine for my lover, my hero, my desert date!

(Both now sing their respective songs in counterpoint, while HAND-MAIDEN hurries on with goblet of wine and hands it to SAMSON; the instant song is ended, he drinks, blinks, then sinks onto the chaise — his head high enough to clear the back-support — and passes out.)

HANDMAIDEN. You really mix a terrific mickey! Shall I call in the Philistine soldiers to slay him, mistress?

DELILAH. No. No soldiers. I need some barbers. We're going to give Samson a haircut.

HANDMAIDEN. Say, the heat *really* got to you, didn't it!

DELILAH. Don't be impertinent! Fetch those barbers at once! *(HANDMAIDEN hurries off.)* Ah, Samson, Samson! So big and strong — and soon to be as helpless as a baby, and the Philistines will pay me a fortune when I turn you over to them!

SATAN. *(Pops onstage immediately.)* What's this? Betrayal? Greed? Treachery? This is my kind of territory!

(HANDMAIDEN hurries in with two BARBERS.)

HANDMAIDEN. These were all I could find on short notice, Mistress.

DELILAH. One would have been enough — but with two, the job will go twice as fast. Hurry, now, and get his head shorn before he wakens!

BARBER. What's the big rush?

DELILAH. If he wakens before you're through, he will slay us all!

BARBER #2. But — if he awakens with no hair on his head — he's likely to do the same thing!

DELILAH. You don't understand! I have discovered the secret of his strength. It lies in his hair — cut it off, and he will be helpless!

HANDMAIDEN. Oh, Mistress! How could I have doubted your sanity for a moment!

BARBER. A mere woman — conquering the strongest man in history!

BARBER #2. You are terrific, with a capital T!

(BARBERS poise their scissors [yes, scissors are an anachronism, but they look more barberish than single blades], and SATAN and HAND-MAIDEN move to stand beside them, the BARBERS behind SAMSON'S head, SATAN and HANDMAIDEN each near one of his shoulders.)

QUARTET. *(singing a capella)*
DELILAH, NOBODY CAN RESIST YOU!
A GUY TURNS TO MUD ONCE HE HAS KISSED YOU!
WHOEVER DARES ROMANCE YOU IS IN FOR A FALL;
HE HASN'T GOT A CHANCE TO SUBDUE YOU AT ALL!
(They gesture to SAMSON.)
DELILAH, YOU TAUGHT HIM QUITE A LESSON!
THIS GUY SHOULDN'T OUGHT TO HAVE BEEN MESSIN'
WITH THE QUEEN OF THE VAMPS, THE CHAMPION OF CHAMPS,
AND THE SCOURGE OF ANY MEN WHO TRY TO RILE YA—
DELILAH! OH, WHAT A GAL!

(As they sustain final chord of barbershop harmony, stage lights go to black, but backdrop remains lighted, so that we can see BARBERS in silhouette as they pantomime start of haircutting; DELILAH moves up closer to them to watch, and SATAN moves downstage to speak heavenward.)

SATAN. Ha! The hero of the Israelites! Helpless! How do you like *them* apples?!

GOD. It is all in keeping with my plan.

SATAN. What? It can't be! The Philistines still hold Israel in thralldom! And the one man who could have saved your people is helpless!

GOD. Oh, yes. And once his hair is shorn, they'll blind him, just to be on the safe side. And he will repent his flouting of his own vows to me, and become the humble servant of the Lord that he was meant to be, before his superhuman strength made him over-confident and promiscuous.

SATAN. A fine ending for a formerly great hero! I love it! Blind and weak and helpless — he'll die in disgrace, an everlasting shame to his people!

GOD. Oh — not quite.

(Backdrop now starts fading and dimming.)

SATAN. What do you mean?

GOD. In the autumn they will take him to the temple of their idol, Dagon, to mock and humiliate him before all their wicked nation during their harvest festival. There will be more Philistines in that temple than all he slew when he had his sight and strength. And they shall bind him to the two pillars upon which the entire vault of the temple rests. Imagine — if those pillars should be moved — the whole thing would come down upon the Philis-tines.... Ka-powee!

SATAN. Oh, no! You wouldn't!

GOD. Oh, wouldn't I!

SATAN. But — that's not fair! He'll die in total glory, destroying his enemies with his last act! His name will be revered forever!

GOD. I keep telling you — I never lose.

(SATAN gives a roar of impotent rage.)

BLACKOUT

ACT TWO
Scene Two

Stage lights and backdrop — a cottage interior — come up. A middle-aged WOMAN and her MOTHER are seated on a low bench.)

WOMAN. That husband of mine! He's been gone for weeks, and not a word from him!

MOTHER. Daughter, it's your own fault! I *told* you to marry a nice doctor, but would you listen? No!

WOMAN. And this isn't the *first* time he's done this! He's *always* going off someplace or other, and makes the dopiest excuses when he gets home!

MOTHER. You can't trust a man like that! Men always lie to stay out of trouble!

WOMAN. I remember the first time he ran off! Showed up a week later, and claimed he'd been held prisoner by bandits!

MOTHER. And what about the time he was gone a month, and then he claimed he'd had amnesia and couldn't remember where he lived?!

WOMAN. Or the time he said a giant bird had carried him off to another country, and he had to hitchhike home!

MOTHER. I'll never forget the time he said a witch turned him into a frog, and it took three weeks for him to break the spell!

WOMAN. Well, I'll tell you one thing, Mother — when he comes home *this* time, he'd better have a believable story, or I'm going to pound his head with the frying pan!

MOTHER. Men never change! Ten to one, he'll have still *another* cock-and-bull story, and expect you to swallow it!

WOMAN. Not this time! If he doesn't have a believable excuse, he's gonna be in *big* trouble!

MOTHER. *(Stands, points offstage.)* Look! There he comes now!

WOMAN. *(Stands, looks.)* And he's smiling! How dare he smile after such a long absence!

MOTHER. I'll bet his story is gonna be a beaut!
WOMAN. Mother, you go get the frying pan, just in case!
MOTHER. Now you're talking!

(MOTHER exits left, as HUSBAND enters right; he smiles uncertainly at his wife, and just stands there.)

WOMAN. *(She folds her arms and speaks.)* Okay! You're home! And what's the big fish story *this* time, Jonah?!

(HUSBAND turns a mournfully helpless gaze out at us, and holds it two seconds, and we go to—)

BLACKOUT

ACT TWO
Scene Three

Lights come up on royal palace interior; BATHSHEBA enters with HANDMAIDEN; a MYRMIDON enters opposite.

BATHSHEBA. Good morning.

MYRMIDON. Ah, good morning, milady. Can I help you?

BATHSHEBA. Yes. I'd like to see King David. It's most urgent.

MYRMIDON. I believe he's in his council chambers. But I'll see what I can do. *(Exits the way he entered.)*

HANDMAIDEN. Oh, sweet Bathsheba — what's to become of you?!

BATHSHEBA. I don't know, truly I don't. The penalty for adultery is stoning. Even the king himself cannot change that law.

HANDMAIDEN. It's all Uriah's fault!

BATHSHEBA. My husband? How do you figure? *He* hasn't committed adultery, *I* have. With King David.

HANDMAIDEN. Yes, but if Uriah hadn't made that foolish vow to refrain from sex until this war is won, your husband would think the child was his own — as matters stand, he'll *know* it's someone else's!

BATHSHEBA. Don't I know it! Ah well, the only thing to do is lay the problem before David — after all, he's as much to blame as I am. Maybe he can figure an out for me.

HANDMAIDEN. And if he cannot?

BATHSHEBA. Don't be a defeatist. David will think of something, I just know he will!

HANDMAIDEN. You amaze me, milady, the way in which you remain optimistic in the face of certain doom — how do you do it?

BATHSHEBA. Easy. I just keep giving myself pep-talks. Like this: *(Music intros, and she sings.)*

HEY, BATHSHEBA, YOU'RE NOT DONE FOR!

JUST MAY BE THE CROWN YOU'VE WON, FOR,
DAVID'S HEART IS HOT FOR YOU!
TIED UP IN A KNOT FOR YOU!
HEY, BATHSHEBA! WHAT A FUTURE
LIES AHEAD IF YOU RECRUIT YOUR
TALENT FOR ATTRACTIVENESS!
GAL, YOUR SHEER DISTRACTIVENESS
ENTHRALLS HIM
AS YOUR BEAUTY BEFALLS HIM!
KINGLY DUTY APPALLS HIM WHEN YOU'RE NEAR!
KEEP ON PITCHING!
YOU'RE BEWITCHING!
HEY, BATHSHEBA! TURN THE HEAT ON!
TEACH HIM TO BE INDISCREET ON
EACH OCCASION WHEN YOU MEET!
USE PERSUASION, DEAR!
JUST STROKE HIS HAIR,
TELL HIM HOW MUCH YOU CARE,
HOW MUCH YOU WANT HIM THERE
RIGHT AT YOUR SIDE!
MOVE IN AND CHUCK HIS CHIN,
TELL HIM THE MESS YOU'RE IN,
AND WHEN YOU CLAIM YOU'RE GAME
TO BE HIS BRIDE...
IT'S CUT-AND-DRIED!

HANDMAIDEN. I do admire your high spirits, milady. But aren't you carrying optimism a little too far? Be thankful if you get out from under the sentence of death — don't also aspire to share the throne!

BATHSHEBA. But what else can David do? The child is his — he will want it raised in royalty — and that can only happen if I live here with him in the palace.

HANDMAIDEN. But the king already has a wife.

BATHSHEBA. *(Shrugs.)* So he'll take on a spare. Why not? A king can get away with it.

(DAVID enters.)

BATHSHEBA. Oh there you are, at last!

DAVID. My darling, you should not be here! We have just had a war council, and I have sent for your husband, Uriah! He'll be here at any moment. If he should find you here—

BATHSHEBA. David, we have bigger problems than that! Remember when you looked from the palace and saw me bathing?

DAVID. How could I forget?

BATHSHEBA. And you sent for me, and I came up here, and one thing led to another, and—

DAVID. Yes-yes, I remember all that.

BATHSHEBA. Well, your little investment in love is paying a dividend in about eight months!

DAVID. What?! But — your husband has taken a vow — he'll never believe it's his!

BATHSHEBA. Right! Any ideas?

DAVID. I don't know. If there were some way to make Uriah *break* his vow, he would think the child was his own...

BATHSHEBA. That's *it*! Oh, what a quick thinker you are! But — how can you get him to break it? If you *order* him to, he might get suspicious.

DAVID. True. I shall have to be subtle! Ah! I have it! A dance! A subtle, enticing, erotic dance! That will put him in the mood for love, and when I send him *home* to you, thus inclined—!

BATHSHEBA. It'll be a snap! You get him hot, and I put the fire to good use!

DAVID. Myrmidon! Bring two cushions, at once!

MYRMIDON. *(off)* At once, sire!

DAVID. It's nice to be obeyed without question.

HANDMAIDEN. He wouldn't be a myrmidon if he didn't. A myrmidon's *function* is to obey orders without question, no matter what!

BATHSHEBA. But what are the cushions *for*, David?

DAVID. Uriah and I shall sit upon them, and I shall talk to him of the joys of the bedchamber while the dancing girl heats up his blood!

HANDMAIDEN. Shall I go get a dancing girl for you?

BATHSHEBA. No! I have a better idea! After all, this girl *must* remind him of his *wife*, right? Well, what better reminder for him, then, than *me*? Quick, give me your veil!

HANDMAIDEN. Yes, milady! *(Hands it over.)*

(BATHSHEBA puts it on, and exits.)

DAVID. Here comes Uriah! Let's hope our scheme works!

HANDMAIDEN. I'll go get the band warmed up! *(Exits in direction MYRMIDON spoke from.)*

URIAH. *(A moment later, enters from opposite side.)* Hail, my king! I wanted to report to you about the progress of the war!

DAVID. Oh, what an unfortunate time, Uriah! I was just about to audition a new dancing girl!

URIAH. Is not the war more important, sire?

DAVID. Well, actually, I must confess, I wanted *you* to see her dance.

(MYRMIDON will enter with two large cushions — the square kind, about two feet on a side, with tassels hanging from each corner, would be best — and place them side-by-side upstage center, then exit, during:)

DAVID. War isn't easy. You could use the relaxation.

URIAH. Oh, but sire, you need not arrange diversion for me! Let us go to the council chamber and discuss the war! *(Starts off.)*

DAVID. *(Stops him.)* Hold, my friend! I *have* arranged a little diversion for you!

(Music intros, and DAVID leads URIAH to cushions, they sit down; BATH-SHEBA, in veil, enters, bows to DAVID, and begins an alluring dance; remainder of DAVID/URIAH dialogue is over music, during dance.)

URIAH. *(Rises.)* Sire—!

DAVID. Dally but a moment!

URIAH. *(Sits again, reluctantly.)* I must remind you, sire—!

DAVID. Hush! Observe the dance!

URIAH. I must not dwell upon carnal imaginings.

DAVID. Observe!

URIAH. But—!

DAVID. Has ever woman radiated such alluring promise of blissful delight?

URIAH. Truly she is of a surpassing charm, my lord. But I am bound to my vow!

DAVID. Uriah, do not persist! I *release* you from your vow!

URIAH. You are most kind, sire, but I have vowed, vowed before the Lord!

DAVID. Friend, I pray you, abandon this mortification of your flesh!

URIAH. I must focus my entire energy upon the winning of your holy war!

DAVID. Reflect upon the joys that await even now in your own bedchamber!

URIAH. Sire, I have vowed. I shall not break that holy vow!

DAVID. *(desperately)* But, *gaze* upon her, Uriah! Her form, her movements, her erotic warmth—!

URIAH. *(Rises.)* Sire, I truly *must* return to the battlefront! I pray you excuse me! *(He exits just as last chord of the dance plays.)*

DAVID. *(over the ominous chording of new music)* The fool. The gallant young fool! Uriah — must die!

BATHSHEBA. *(just removing veil) Die*, my lord?

DAVID. Would you rather be stoned?

BATHSHEBA. ...No, my lord.

DAVID. Then *he* must die!

(Music climaxes and stops.)

DAVID. Once dead, he can no longer disclaim the paternity of your child! Myrmidon!

MYRMIDON. *(Enters, bows.)* What is your will, majesty?

DAVID. I have a mission for you of gravest urgency.

MYRMIDON. Speak, sire, and it shall be accomplished.

DAVID. Uriah is about to leave for the battlefront. Tell his companion, who travels with him, this message. At the next battle, when Uriah is in the thick of the fighting, the rest of the troops are to draw back and leave him alone there, amongst the enemy. Understood?

MYRMIDON. Understood, sire! *(Salutes and exits in direction URIAH took.)*

BATHSHEBA. A foul trick upon a fine man.

DAVID. Upon a man whose only crime was his loyalty to his sovereign. But why dwell upon it? *(Music intros, and he sings.)*
IT IS DONE.

BATHSHEBA. *(In a cheerier mood than DAVID, sings.)*
I SHALL LIVE!

DAVID. *(Sings.)*
ALL IS WELL, AND NO LONGER NEED WE DWELL
ON THE FATE THAT WAS DUE FOR OUR SIN HITHER-
TO!

BATHSHEBA. *(Overlapping his words with her own, sings.)*
I SHALL GIVE YOU THANKS EVERMORE!
WE CAN IGNORE FATEFUL DOOM THAT WAS DUE TO
ME,
FOR OUR SIN WAS A CHANCE TO BEGET ROMANCE!

DAVID. *(Sings.)*
IT IS DONE. HE SHALL DIE.
NONE SHALL KNOW THAT YOU AND I
SHARE THE BLAME FOR HIS DOOM!

BATHSHEBA. *(Sings.)*
WE'LL SURVIVE! LOVE WILL THRIVE,
I KNOW, DARLING MINE! WHO DARES ASSIGN
BLAME TO US FOR HIS DOOM?
SO, DEAR, LET OUR SHAME NOW DISPEL!

DAVID. *(Sings.)*
LET OUR SHAME BE HIS TOMB!

BATHSHEBA. *(Sings.)*
TOMBSTONES NEVER TELL!

DAVID. *(Sings.)*
HIS END SHALL BE ON OUR MINDS
EV'RY TIME WE DRAW A BREATH.

BATHSHEBA. *(Sings.)*
BE NOT SAD! DARLING, EV'RY TIME WE DRAW A
BREATH,
YOU THRILL ME THROUGH! MY LOVE FOR YOU IS
TRUE!

DAVID. *(Sings.)*
THROUGH MY LOVE FOR YOU, I NOW MUST REPENT
THAT I HAVE SENT A FRIEND TO CERTAIN DEATH!

BATHSHEBA. *(Sings.)*
I NEVER MEANT TO CIRCUMVENT DEATH,
BUT NOW I KNOW LIFE IS WORTH THE WOE!
DAVID. *(Sings.)*
I STOLE ANOTHER'S WIFE, THEN STOLE HIS LIFE
TO SAVE HER FROM THE DREADED FATE THE LAW
ALLOWED!
BATHSHEBA. *(Sings.)*
YOU SAVED ME FROM THE DREADED FATE
THE AWFUL LAW ALLOWED,
AND DARLING, I'M SO VERY PROUD!
DAVID. *(Sings.)*
YET NOW, I'M NOT SO PROUD!
MYRMIDON. *(Just as song is completed, re-enters and bows low to DAVID.)* Your will has been accomplished, my lord. The message is given, and Uriah shall be dead before the fall of night.
DAVID. So soon as that! So soon as that! A word from me, and a man is dead!
MYRMIDON. Naturally, sire. You are the king. Your word is life or death.
DAVID. You are dismissed.
MYRMIDON. Good day, then, my lord. *(Exits.)*
DAVID. A king. A royal monarch. The glory of it is not as comforting as one would imagine. I have betrayed a friend— *(Looks wearily at BATHSHEBA.)* —and what have I won in exchange? The love of a woman already proven to be unreliable in matters of love and trust. *(Sings.)*
WHAT HAVE I DONE? WHAT HAVE I WON?
THE DREADFUL DEED I DECREED DID DETER
FIT PUNISHMENT FOR HER!
TO THE THRONE SHE'LL ASCEND
AT THE COST OF A FRIEND.
THROUGH SELFISH PRIDE A MAN HAS DIED.
HIS SACRIFICE WAS THE PRICE THAT WAS PAID
BY FRIENDSHIP I BETRAYED!
AND THE PLOT I'D BEGUN
NOW CANNOT BE UNDONE!

(Throughout, BATHSHEBA scarcely pays attention; her mood has been brightening by the minute, and now, as DAVID repeats his mournful song, she contrapuntally sings.)

BATHSHEBA. *(Sings.)*
I'M GONNA BE A QUEEN, BEDECKED IN SATIN AND LACE!
WITH SERVANTS, HANDMAIDENS, AND JOOLERY!
HEAVEN KNOWS I HAVE BEEN THROUGH ENOUGH
TO GAIN THE THRONE! WHO CARES IF MY BLOOD IS NOT BLUE ENOUGH?
I WEAR HIS RING!
I'M GONNA BE A QUEEN, A REGAL SMILE ON MY FACE!
INDULGING IN ROYAL TOMFOOLERY!
RUNNING THE ARMY AND NAVY, TOO—
AND I WILL TRY TO GIVE A FEW MOMENTS TO DAVY-POO!
OUR LOVE WILL BE SUBLIME
WHEN I CAN SPARE THE TIME

(And as DAVID gives her a woeful look of misery—)

BLACKOUT

ACT TWO
Scene Four

We hear in the darkness:

SATAN. I must say, you sure can pick 'em! That David — what a rotten trick he played upon poor, noble Uriah!

GOD. Don't get carried away. Uriah wasn't *that* noble. No husband or wife should ever deprive the other of conjugal rights without the other's consent — there's no nobility in that. His loyalty to the king was admirable — but his first loyalty should have been to his wife.

SATAN. Then you *approve* of David's deed?

GOD. Of course not. Destroying a life is worse than cuckolding a mate. No, what David did was completely dishonorable. But of course, he repented later.

SATAN. Still and all, with a setup like that, very little good will come out of the house of David!

GOD. Don't be so sure of that. There will be someone in the line of David's house that will supercede any good man before or after him.

SATAN. Prophecies, prophecies! Don't you ever give up? All your people ever get out of life is a boot in the rear! Look at Daniel, your true prophet! For speaking your word, he's going to be devoured by lions! He ought to wise up and change his ways and save his neck!

GOD. Do you think he can be persuaded to do so?

SATAN. Men are foolish. They can be persuaded to turn away from you with almost no effort on *my* part at *all*!

GOD. Let us *see* what you can do about Daniel...

(Stage lights come up, and backdrop is now a craggy interior as befits a lions' den carved into rocky ground; DANIEL, hands clasped in prayer, kneels there, eyes heavenward; SATAN is standing beside him.)

DANIEL. Lord, I'm not too crazy about being chewed up alive —
so if you will, spare me that fate when the lions are let in here — but
if you won't — well, that's all right too. Your will is my will.

SATAN. Daniel! Daniel, get up and look at me!

DANIEL. *(Startled, gets to his feet.)* Who are you? Another victim for
the hungry lions?

SATAN. Let's just say I'm a friend. A friend who can get you out
of here!

DANIEL. Out of the lions' den? Oh, I'd be most grateful for
that!

SATAN. Grateful enough to renounce your Lord?

DANIEL. What? Oh, no, I could never desert my Lord's
service.

SATAN. Why not? *He's* certainly deserted *you*! Look at the spot
you're in! And him master of the universe! Don't be a dope!
Renounce him, and I'll get you out of here!

DANIEL. Never! He has *not* deserted me! He may do with me as
He wills! *(Music intros, and he sings.)*
I KNOW THE LORD WILL REMAIN BY MY SIDE
WHATEVER BECOMES OF ME.
I HAVE IMPLORED HIM TO HELP ME ABIDE
WHATEVER MUST COME TO BE.
YOUR EMPTY WORDS DON'T DECEIVE ME;
LEAVE ME! I DIE CONTENTEDLY.
TO MY REWARD I SHALL GO SATISFIED,
FOR DYING WILL SET ME FREE
TO LOVE HIM ETERNALLY.

SATAN. *(Furious he sings.)*
ALL RIGHT! THAT'S HOW YOU FEEL!
YOU'RE GONNA MAKE A TASTY LITTLE MEAL!

*(He beckons, and instantly three LIONESSES with cheerleader pompoms
       enter [these are three women in body stockings, with lion-ear caps and
       tails, and cat-whiskered faces] and they crouch with hungry looks at
       DANIEL as —much like a pep-rally cheer-leader — SATAN
       sings.)*

SATAN. *(Sings.)*

ROAR, LIONS, ROAR!

(*TRIO does roar-roar-roar like rah-rah-rah.*)

SATAN. (*Sings.*)
HERE'S THE APPETIZER YOU'VE BEEN WAITING FOR!
THOUGH HE LOOKS A LITTLE THIN,
YOU HAD BETTER DIG RIGHT IN,
THERE'S NO TELLING WHEN YOU'RE GETTING ANY
MORE!
SCRATCH, LIONS, SCRATCH!

(*TRIO does triple "scratch!" same way.*)

SATAN. (*Sings.*)
TILL HIS ARMS AND LEGS AND FINGERS YOU DETACH!
PILE THE PIECES HERE AND THERE
TILL THE DISTRIBUTION'S FAIR,
AND YOU SETTLE DOWN TO DINING WITH DISPATCH!
DANIEL. (*Sings.*)
I WILL NOT RUN; YOUR WILL BE DONE!
SATAN. (*Even more furiously, sings.*)
KILL, LIONS, KILL!
TRIO. (*Sings.*)
KILL, KILL, KILL!
SATAN. (*Sings.*)
HE IS TOUGH, BUT QUITE ENOUGH TO FILL THE BILL!
THOUGH HE'S THIN, YOU CAN REJOICE:
ALL THE MEAT ON HIM IS CHOICE—
IT'S A WASTE TO TALK OF TASTINESS UNTIL—
(*Shout-chants over music:*)
—he's through the lips and over the gums;
Look out, stomach, here he comes!
(*Sings again.*)
DON'T RETREAT, IT'S TIME TO EAT YOUR FILL!

(*There is a loud thunderclap; SATAN panics and runs off, while TRIO of
    lionesses cower and cover their eyes.*)

GOD. Daniel, you are saved. Your unswerving loyalty cannot be punished by these animals. Lions, depart!

(TRIO gratefully scurry away.)

GOD. Rest now, Daniel. The danger is past. Soon your captors will see that you have been spared, and they will release you from the pit, and hurl in those persons who plotted against your life, instead. And this time, the lions *will* be fed!

(As DANIEL makes following speech, backdrop will fade to black, and stage lights — excepting one bright spotlight on him — will also dim to black.)

DANIEL. *(Raises his eyes heavenward, and raises his hands in praise.)* My God has sent His angel and has shut up the mouths of the lions, and they have not hurt me, since before Him justice has been found in me. My God is the living and eternal God forever, and His Kingdom shall not be destroyed, and His power shall be forever. He is the deliverer and savior, doing signs and wonders in heaven and on earth. Lo, one like the son of man shall come with the clouds of heaven, and shall be given power and glory and a kingdom, and all peoples, tribes and tongues shall serve Him. His power is an everlasting power that shall not be taken away, and His kingdom shall not be destroyed henceforth!

BLACKOUT

ACT TWO
Scene Five

In the darkness, we hear:

SATAN. And so it goes, year in, year out, day-by-day, century after century! Adam and Eve thrust out into the cold world beyond the garden — Noah's family bobbing about on that ark in cramped and smelly quarters — Abraham suffering the dread of sacrificing his son — Lot losing his wife to her curiosity — Esau losing his birthright — Moses disappointed in the faith of his followers — Joshua having to fight for the Promised Land — Samson being blinded and destroying his enemies along with himself — the list is endless. You wonder why your followers desert you? Who would *not* desert you?! Your laws are too hard, the rewards too few. You ask far too much of your followers. It is no wonder they do not obey!

GOD. What if I were to tell you that there is one person of whom I ask even more? One person who shall suffer everything that anyone on earth ever has suffered or ever will suffer, and who shall remain faithful to me, regardless?

SATAN. You are joking, of course. Such a one cannot be.

GOD. Let me tell you about him, Satan. His mother shall know the sense of disgrace felt by all unwed mothers ... he shall be born in poverty, and of a minority race, and in a veritible police state ... then he and his family will have to flee their homeland to an alien country ... he shall lose his earthly father at a youthful age and be his mother's only support ... later, he shall go about speaking of peace and love and goodness and truth — and for his reward, he shall be abandoned by his followers — shall be betrayed by a close friend — shall be falsely accused of a crime he did not commit — shall be tortured and beaten up by the hoodlum followers of the ruling tyrant — and shall be put to death, shamefully, in a public place, before his own mother's eyes. And yet — at no moment in his entire life — not even once — shall he ever fail to obey my every wish, and do so joyfully, and never falter in his love and devotion and trust in me!

SATAN. Such a one is impossible! It cannot be done.

GOD. What kind of a God would I be if I demanded of my followers more than I was willing to undergo myself!?

SATAN. Yourself? Undergo *yourself?*

GOD. And henceforth, when my followers shall say, "It is hard, Lord. It cannot be done!", I shall reply, "It can be done. I have done it. I have shown you the way. *I* am the way!"

SATAN. What are you talking about, *you* showing the way? *You* suffering all those torments? *You* setting an example for your followers? When is all this supposed to come to pass, anyhow?

GOD. It is already come to pass. It happens even now. And neither you nor any other power in creation can stop it!

SATAN. Now? Happening now? Where?

GOD. In Bethlehem of Judea.

(Stage lights come up; backdrop is a mass of dark sky and stars, and one spectacularly large star; the stable, with MARY, JOSEPH, the baby, and any mixture of persons you want [Wise Men, shepherds, angels, whatever] in the scene are there, all looking toward the baby, and all singing a capella.*)*

CHORUS. *(Sings.)*
LULLABY, SWEET JESUS, LAY DOWN YOUR DROWSY HEAD.
SHEPHERDS KEEP THEIR VIGIL BY YOUR MANGER BED.
ANGELS HOVER NEAR YOU AND WATCH WHERE YOU LAY..
LULLABY, SWEET JESUS, BE WITH US NOW WE PRAY.

SATAN. *(Furious, starts dancing in and out among the group, none of whom pay any heed as he sings.)*
WHY SHOULD YOU ADORE THE INFANT?
YOU PEOPLE ARE REALLY DUMB!
DON'T TELL ME YOU BUY THE RIDICULOUS LIE
A MINUSCULE MESSIAH HAS COME?!
WHY SHOULD YOU ADORE THE INFANT?

HOW CAN YOU BELIEVE THIS JUNK?
DON'T QUAKE IN SUBMISSION! HAVE YOU NO SUSPI-
CION
IT'S ALL SUPERSTITIONAL BUNK?!
Sees he's making no impression, muses aloud:)
THEY SOMEHOW SEEM TO UNDERSTAND
HOW MIGHTY THIS BABY COULD BE.
I'VE GOT TO GET THE UPPER HAND
OR HE'LL GET THE BETTER OF ME!
(to the group again)
WHY SHOULD YOU ADORE THE INFANT?
HE'S DOING AWAY WITH SIN!
HE'LL MAKE YOU REPENT AND YOU'LL COME TO RE-
SENT
THE PREDICAMENT HE'S PUT YOU IN!
I'M WARNING YOU, SOON YOU'LL BE DONE
WITH ALL GAIETY, LAUGHTER AND FUN!
WHY SHOULD YOU ADORE THE INFANT—?

(Chorus starts repeating their melody wordlessly, on the syllable "Oh...", des-
pite SATAN'S roars and growls of rage, until:)

SATAN. *(Over music — he rages, crossing his arms before his face, and backing from the light.)* Oh, hell! It's all over, he's won! *(Wails hideously and rushes off.)*
CHORUS. *(louder and happier)*
LULLABY, SWEET JESUS, A CHILD AND YET A KING.
PROMISE OF SALVATION TO EARTH NOW YOU BRING.
MAN HAS WANDERED FAR FROM YOUR FATHER ABOVE.
STAY WITH US, SWEET JESUS, OUR BLESSED GIFT OF
LOVE!

(And as they sustain final chord, stage lights dim swiftly to black, and the last
thing we see are the sky and that bright shining star in it, as—)

THE CURTAIN FALLS

END OF SHOW

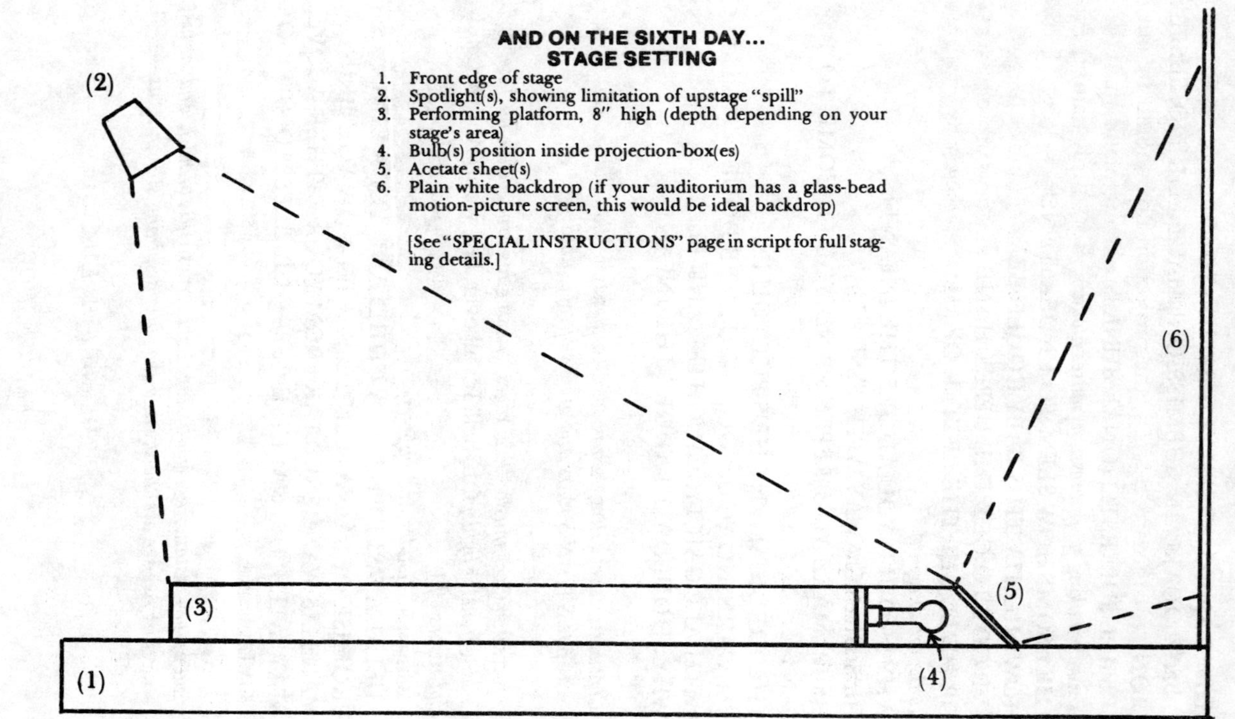

AND ON THE SIXTH DAY...
STAGE SETTING
1. Front edge of stage
2. Spotlight(s), showing limitation of upstage "spill"
3. Performing platform, 8" high (depth depending on your stage's area)
4. Bulb(s) position inside projection-box(es)
5. Acetate sheet(s)
6. Plain white backdrop (if your auditorium has a glass-bead motion-picture screen, this would be ideal backdrop)
[See "SPECIAL INSTRUCTIONS" page in script for full staging details.]
(1)
(2)
(3)
(4)
(5)
(6)

SPECIAL INSTRUCTIONS

The multiple sets indicated in the script are accomplished by the simple expedient of a distortion-projection on a rear white backdrop (see *STAGE SETTING* for illustration). This is simplicity itself to construct. Ideally, the projection-box should be out of audience-view behind a raised (8 inch) playing-platform. If this is not feasible, there are two alternatives: (1.) Simply paint the top and downstage faces of the box in a neutral color — say, the same as the stage floor itself — and let the audience (and audiences are always generous in such matters) simply ignore its presence; or (2.) if you have the facilities, use a translucent backdrop and *rear-*project the settings upon it.

As with a Mercator-Projection of the globe, the images from the translucent-paint drawings upon the acetate distort at their widening-angle of light. To pre-compensate for the distortion (It can be done mathematically, but this is a real grind), simply place opaque objects upon the face of a clear sheet of acetate and move them about until the desired positioning upon the backdrop is achieved, mark their positions on the acetate, then paint them in with translucent colors. (For instance, the palace scene in the David/Bathsheba segment: If you opt for tall marble pillars in the background, lay a half-dozen-or-so pencils upon the acetate and move them until their projected shadows are vertical [you will discover that a teepee-shape arrangement of the pencils produces a parallel-vertical arrangement of the shadows], outline their positions, and then paint them in with marbleized streaks, etc.)

If you want to be really ambitious, in scenes such as when Abraham/Isaac are going up to the mountain, or Lot and his group are fleeing Sodom and Gomorrah, you might have a *sliding* segment of acetate move across the box in the opposite direction to that in which the players are moving (that is, *apparently* moving; we must have them "walk in place" so they don't exit the stage, with or without a moving projection), for a true visual treat.

The only "real" settings in the show are in the first and final scenes — the propriety-necessitated "hedges" to hide the no-no parts of Adam and Eve, and a "real" stable for the Nativity scene, (It can be behind the backdrop, which can be removed for this final scene, to show that we are out of the "dim past" and into the "real present-day era.").

NOTES ON THE WORLD PREMIERE PRODUCTION

The cast and crew decided that the show was strong enough to do *without* any rear-projection backgrounds, and that's how they performed it, using only minimal props, as follows:

1. Adam and Eve, of course, *had* that necessary shrubbery (cardboard flats painted with leaves) between them and the audience for their segment.

2. For Noah's scene, they had a low foreground of ship's side-planking (cardboard again) between players and audience.

3. For Abraham's two scenes, they used only the single chair, as specified in the script; he and young Isaac "marched in place" for their mountain-climbing sequence.

4. Sodom and Gomorrah: No scenery at all, but they used that sudden salt-whitening spotlight upon Lot's wife for her transformation scene, and the audience gasped and applauded, as the actress froze in place, a shocked look on her face, until the lights faded on the scene.

5. For the Jericho scene, they decided to play the scene facing *downstage*, as if the Walls of Jericho loomed between them and the audience — then, at the final trumpet-blast, they "watched the walls crumble" by eye-and-head indications, so that one could almost *see* the devastation they pretended to be witnessing.

6. For the Samson scene, they used a chaise lounge for Delilah to loll and pout upon, and for Samson to collapse upon later, before the barbershop quartet entered.

7. For David's scene, they had a huge double-seater throne upstage right, angled to face downstage left, upon which David and Uriah viewed Bathsheba's futile dancing.

8. For Daniel's scene, they had a section of "prison-cell type" bars upstage between slightly parted curtains, with no lionesses visible until Satan opens the door and admits them; the lionesses fled back into this "cell" when the thunder crashed.

9. For the final scene, they opened the upstage curtains to reveal an open-fronted stable, with the whole cast doubling as angels, shepherds, the Magi, etc., flanking the scene. The final "Lullaby," after Satan flees, got a standing ovation.

HOME-BUILT

Lighting Equipment
for The Small Stage
By THEODORE FUCHS

This volume presents a series of fourteen simplified designs for building various types of stage lighting and control equipment, with but one purpose in mind—to enable the amateur producer to acquire a complete set of stage lighting equipment at the lowest possible cost. The volume is 8½" x 11" in size, with heavy paper and spiral binding—features which make the volume well suited to practical workshop use.

Community Theatre
A MANUAL FOR SUCCESS
By JOHN WRAY YOUNG

The ideal text for anyone interested in participating in Community Theatre as a vocation or avocation. "Organizing a Community Theatre," "A Flight Plan for the Early Years," "Programming for People—Not Computers," and other chapters are blueprints for solid growth. "Technical, Business and Legal Procedures" cuts a safe and solvent path through some tricky undergrowth. Essential to the library of all community theatres, and to the schools who will supply them with talent in the years to come.

HERE'S HOW

A Basic Stagecraft Book

THOROUGHLY REVISED
AND ENLARGED

by HERBERT V. HAKE

COVERING 59 topics on the essentials of stagecraft (13 of them brand new). *Here's How* meets a very real need in the educational theater. It gives to directors and others concerned with the technical aspects of play production a complete and graphic explanation of ways of handling fundamental stagecraft problems.

The book is exceptional on several counts. It not only treats every topic thoroughly, but does so in an easy-to-read style every layman can understand. Most important, it is prepared in such a way that for every topic there is a facing page of illustrations (original drawings and photographs)—thus giving the reader a complete graphic presentation of the topic along with the textual description of the topic.

Because of the large type, the large size of the pages (9″ x 12″), and the flexible metal binding, *Here's How* will lie flat when opened and can be laid on a workbench for a director to read while in a *standing* position.

Bible Herstory

PATRICIA MONTLEY

(May Double.) Satire.

18 females—Bare Stage

Bible Herstory, a one-act feminist satire in six scenes featuring an all-woman cast. In "Paradise Abandoned," Eve convinces God not to stifle Her creativity just because She made a mistake in creating Adam. In "Noah's Ark-itect," Noah's wife and daughter prepare for the flood and "inspire" Noah to build a boat. "The Sacrifice of Sarah" shows Abraham's wife working on a theatrical project to save a lazy Isaac's life. In "Miriam in Labor," Moses' sister bargains with Pharaoh's daughter for better working conditions. In "Queen Solomon and the Paternity Suit," her Majesty proposes to cut in half a philandering charioteer claimed by both wife and mistress. In "The Renunciation," Mary rejects the Angel Gabriella's offer of the saviorship of the world, but agrees to have a son. $2.00.

Out of Our Father's House

Play with music. (All Groups.)

BASED ON EVE MERRIAM'S
Growing Up Female in America: Ten Lives

3 females play 6 roles
Musicians—1 Interior

Arranged for the stage by Paula Wagner, Jack Hofsiss and Eve Merriam. Music by Ruth Cawford Seeger adapted by Daniel Schrier. With additional music by Daniel Shrier and Marjorie Lipari.

Taken entirely from diaries, journals and letters of the characters portrayed. They are a schoolgirl—founder of the Women's Suffrage Movement, an astronomer, a labor organizer, a minister, a doctor and a woman coming out of the Jewish ghetto. They are watched as they grow up, marry and bear children. They do not covet men's jobs, but when they want careers they are ostracized. A very moving play seen through the words and eyes of 19th century American women. $1.00. Write for information about music.

Other Publications for Your Interest

COMING ATTRACTIONS
(ADVANCED GROUPS—COMEDY WITH MUSIC)

By TED TALLY, music by JACK FELDMAN, lyrics by BRUCE SUSSMAN and FELDMAN

5 men, 2 women—Unit Set

Lonnie Wayne Burke has the requisite viciousness to be a media celebrity—but he lacks vision. When we meet him, he is holding only four people hostage in a laundromat. There aren't any cops much less reporters around, because they're across town where some guy is holding 50 hostages. But, a talent agent named Manny sees possibilities in Lonnie Wayne. He devises a criminal persona for him by dressing him in a skeleton costume and sending him door-to-door, murdering people as "The Hallowe'en Killer". He is captured, and becomes an instant celebrity, performing on TV shows. When his fame starts to wane, he crashes the Miss America Pageant disguised as Miss Wyoming to kill Miss America on camera. However, he falls in love with her, and this eventually leads to his downfall. Lonnie ends up in the electric chair, and is fried "live" on prime-time TV as part of a jazzy production number! "Fizzles with pixilated laughter."—Time. "I don't often burst into gales of laughter in the theatre; here, I found myself rocking with guffaws."—New York Mag. "Vastly entertaining."—Newark Star-Ledger.

SORROWS OF STEPHEN
(ADVANCED GROUPS—COMEDY)

By PETER PARNELL

4 men, 5 women—Unit set

Stephen Hurt is a headstrong, impetuous young man—an irrepressible romantic—he's unable not to be in love. One of his models is Goethe's tragic hero, Werther, but as a contemporary New Yorker, he's adaptable. The end of an apparently undying love is followed by the birth of a grand new passion. And as he believes there's a literary precedent for all romantic possibilities justifying his choices—so with enthusiasm bordering on fickleness, he turns from Tolstoy, to Stendhal or Balzac. And Stephen's never discouraged—he can withstand rivers of rejection. (From the N.Y. Times.) And so his affairs—real and tentative—begin when his girl friend leaves him. He makes a romantic stab at a female cab driver, passes an assignation note to an unknown lady at the opera, flirts with an accessible waitress—and then has a tragic-with-comic-overtones, wild affair with his best friend's fiancée. "Breezy and buoyant. A real romantic comedy, sophisticated and sentimental, with an ageless attitude toward the power of positive love."—N.Y. Times.

Other Publications for Your Interest

THE MAN WITH THE PLASTIC SANDWICH

(LITTLE THEATRE—COMEDY)

By ROGER KARSHNER

2 men, 2 women—Simple exterior

Walter Price, a ''basic blue'' individual, is thrown out of work after twenty years with the same firm. During an anxiety-laden period of job hunting and readjustment Walter attempts to find solace on a bench in an urban park. Here he is confronted by three engaging, provocative characters. First there is Ellie, a high-spirited ingenue who represents hope; then Haley, a distinguished hobo representing wisdom; and finally Lenore, a hooker who represents reality. Each encounter enlightens Walter, gives him perspective, and ultimately new purpose and direction. A very funny play with bittersweet moments and three dimensional characters. ''You will laugh until your sides feel as if they will burst, until your eyes begin to water, until you are sure that one more clever line or witty exchange will send you into a laughing fit from which you may never recover.''—Chicago Sun-Times. ''This play is truly high comedy and I can't think of a soul who wouldn't love the off-beat characters portrayed in this 4-spoked comedic wheel.''—Chicago Reporter/Progress Newspapers.

THE DREAM CRUST

(LITTLE THEATRE—DRAMA)

By ROGER KARSHNER

3 men, 3 women, 1 10-year-old boy —Interior

Named in the Bruns-Mantle Yearbook as one of America's Best Plays. Frank Haynes, an earth-loving farmer, has given up his hound-dogging and high times under the pressure of the family's admonition that ''A man has got to get ahead.'' Haynes would be happy to do nothing but tend his farm and reap whatever profit it might generate. But he realizes that there are five mouths depending on him and the lure of big money available to him in a nearby big-city factory too great to ignore. Set against a backdrop of the land-locked Midwest, the play dramatizes a man's persistent, agonizing search for personal freedom and the sense of loss between father and son. ''A moving portrait of a land-locked family that needs to be seen.''—Variety. ''The plays' spirit, its underlying warmth, particularly in the unspoken father-son relationship, creates a world that's identifiable and that breathes.''—L.A. Herald-Examiner.

HANDBOOK

for

THEATRICAL APPRENTICES

By Dorothy Lee Tompkins

Here is a common sense book on theatre, fittingly subtitled, "A Practical Guide in All Phases of Theatre." Miss Tompkins has wisely left art to the artists and written a book which deals only with the practical side of the theatre. All the jobs of the theatre are categorized, from the star to the person who sells soft drinks at intermission. Each job is defined, and its basic responsibilities given in detail. An invaluable manual for every theatre group in explaining to novices the duties of apprenticeship, and in reassessing its own organizational structure and functions.

"If you are an apprentice or are just aspiring in any capacity, then you'll want to read and own Dorothy Lee Tompkins' A HANDBOOK FOR THEATRICAL APPRENTICES. It should be required reading for any drama student anywhere and is a natural for the amateur in any phase of the theatre."—George Freedley, Morning Telegraph.

"It would be helpful if the HANDBOOK FOR THEATRICAL APPRENTICES were in school or theatrical library to be used during each production as a guide to all participants."—Florence E. Hill, Dramatics Magazine.